Connecting With Your Customers

■ ■ ■

STEVE MORRIS AND
GRAHAM WILLCOCKS

The Institute of Management (IM) is at the forefront of management development and best management practice. The Institute embraces all levels of management from
students to chief executives. It provides a unique portfolio of services for all managers, enabling them to develop skills and achieve management excellence.

If you would like to hear more about the benefits of membership, please write to Department P, Institute of Management, Cottingham Road, Corby NN17 1TT.

This series is commissioned by the Institute of Management Foundation.

PITMAN PUBLISHING
128 Long Acre, London WC2E 9AN

A Division of Pearson Professional Limited

First published in Great Britain 1996

British Library Cataloguing in Publication Data
A CIP catalogue record for this book can be obtained from the British Library.

ISBN 0 273 61685 4

10 9 8 7 6 5 4 3 2 1

Typeset by Northern Phototypesetting Co Ltd, Bolton
Printed and bound in Great Britain by Bell and Bain Ltd, Glasgow

The Publishers' policy is to use paper manufactured from sustainable forests.

About the Authors

■ ■ ■

Steve Morris, director of The Burton Morris Consultancy, is an experienced writer of books, articles and action guides on management. He works with a range of organizations such as The National Consumer Council, Ind Coope, Forte Posthouse and TSB. He is learning consultant for the Institute of Personnel and Development, the University of London and the University of the West Indies.

Graham Willcocks is director of Wesley House Consultancy. He is a writer, trainer and process consultant. He has had wide management experience in both the private and public sectors, developing programmes on leadership, teams, change, customer care and strategic marketing within a wide range of organizations.

Contents

Acknowledgements

The authors would like to thank Sue McKoen for researching and initially drafting some parts of this book. Special thanks also go to Philip Gill and Stephen Connock for their support throughout the various drafts of the book and in particular for contributing their ideas, experience and articles that they have happened upon in their own work.

We would also like to thank the many people who without knowing it have added to the highly practical nature of this book through freely contributing their time and energy to test a number of our approaches in their own organization.

Introduction

■ ■ ■

Staying in tune with customers

This is a book about really getting, and staying, in tune with customers. It has at its very centre the idea that if you make the effort to understand what customers want and orientate your business around this, then you have every chance of keeping your customers for life. And in today's highly competitive business environment, it's the companies that really get in contact with customers and stay in contact with them, that tend to remain in business, and indeed thrive.

All too often, managers lose sight of their customers in the day-to-day business of meeting deadlines or getting the work done. This book stresses that the successful modern manager is the one who continually keeps in touch with customers themselves and works hard to keep their team in tune too.

In many ways lots of the ideas in this book are very simple. The book stresses that it is important to respect customers and have a belief that if you listen to them and stay in contact with them, and develop new ways of strengthening that all-important relationship with them, then they are likely to be loyal and repay your work by giving you their continued custom.

It isn't a traditional book about marketing. It also isn't a book with lots of fancy marketing-type diagrams, bar charts and graphs. In many ways it's a book based on stories and examples which you can take, learn from, and adapt, to suit your own needs. It certainly isn't a book that gets trapped in the marketing-speak and psycho-babble of so many of its competitors.

So, to start the book, we commence with two contrasting stories to bring out many of the points we talk about throughout.

Some people see working in an organization as a slightly prosaic affair. They get hung up on talking about management, control and, of course, bottom line – profitability. Indeed, all these things are important. Companies need managing, and people and products need controlling. And, naturally, the bottom line is always important. But running a successful business is also about listening to customers, and plugging into their dreams and aspirations – however lowly the product you are offering.

Understanding customer decision making

It's a complicated process, deciding on where to place your business. Our choices are based on a whole range of different factors.

Although not all customers think clearly about how they make their decisons, they respond to the way they feel about your business, and the way they feel you think about them. So successful businesses plug into these aspirations, and understand that the experience is everything. Customers are often buying aspirations when they buy a product, and companies would do well to listen to these dreams. For instance when a customer visits a restaurant the food is only one aspect of the decision. They are in fact buying the all-round experience:

- the service
- the atmosphere
- the decor.

And, the sense of being special and belonging.

Aligning your business with customer dreams

Take Budget Rent-a-Car. When one thinks about the High Street rent-a-car business it isn't often with a sense of excitement. More likely we think of fleets of bog standard vehicles.

However, Budget Rent-a-Car have added the legendary US superbike, the Harley Davidson, to its fleet of vehicles. To make a hiring you need to be over thirty and have qualified to ride a motorbike for a minimum of three years, and hold a clean licence. And then, for a mere £99 a day, you can indulge your dreams and hit the road.

Budget decided to add Harleys to its UK fleet after a massive response to its scheme in Germany and Holland. The scheme itself was launched at the beginning of a glorious summer and already queues were building up around the block. So, Budget Rent-a-Car were not constricted by the way they have always done things, and what's more their listening channels were wide open. They listened to customers, and then added a service that would fit in with what customers were looking for. They also made an important statement about themselves as a company. Namely, we are not here just to do what we think is right, we are here to do what you want us to do. They oriented their business around the customer and made a clear statement that the customer is 'king' and that their business was to listen to their aspirations.

Helping customers to feel part of a club

And another example. If you are over thirty, the chances are that when you were growing up you drank bucketfuls of orange squash. It was the staple drink for children, and in many ways one of the defining tastes of our upbringing. Things have changed. These days children are more likely to be drinking a product like Pepsi Max. And in this change we can see a more fundamental change in the way companies have striven to get closer and closer to customers. Pepsi Max is an interesting product. It only costs around 30p a can to buy, and is a classic of mass produced products. It tastes and looks the same throughout the world. It is just a fizzy drink.

However, if you buy a Pepsi Max you are buying into much more than just a soft drink.

For a start there are the adverts. These are fast action, quick cut adverts that have stressed the excitement of the product and urge consumers to 'LIVE LIFE TO THE MAX'.

In this sense they are making a point that this isn't simply a soft drink, it's about buying into a way of life. But the identification between the product and the customer goes even deeper than this.

Currently, if you buy a Pepsi Max you can enter a competition. The winners go to the Pepsi Max Club in Florida free of charge.

When you get to the Club you have a chance to play tennis with stars like Andre Agassi, meet people in the entertainment world like Pamela Anderson, or practise karate with Claude Van Damme.

The company is clearly hoping to make today's youngsters feel that they and the company have some kind of relationship, and something in common. Pepsi are encouraging people to buy into a dream about their product, and are reflecting this back in the range of incentives of gifts and offers that are on the table. So the humble orange squash, the one we picked up from the supermarket, has really been replaced by a lifestyle. There is a good deal of cynicism about this, and indeed some of it is well placed. However, the point remains that a company like Pepsi has tried to break out of its traditional role as a simple mass market producer, and reinvented itself with its product as a part of people's lives. Companies are increasingly realizing that if you don't keep in contact with customers and don't build up this on-going relationship, then a competitor will sneak in and steal their customers away from them.

This book looks at how you can keep your customers for life, and help them feel a part of your business and help your business feel in tune with them. In order to do this, it explains a set of techiques for hanging onto customers for life. These include:

- listening to them – everything from welcoming complaints to setting up listening panels
- learning from customers
- keeping the listening going
- carrying out simple market research
- developing an on-going relationship with customers
- getting your staff attitudes and skills right.

Later in the book, from Chapters 5 to 7 we look at a radical approach to making the customer connection. It is one that may change the whole way you work and shake up many of the things you have always believed to be true. We call this approach:

Welcoming the Death of Marketing.

1

Carrying out some simple market research

Finding out what customers want

Any successful and sustainable organization has to follow a simple formula. Deliver to the customers what they want, consistently, in a way that pleases them and makes them want to come back … and bring a friend. The point of this book is to move beyond traditional marketing approaches and focus on more personal relationships with customers – but you can't build that edifice until the foundations are in place.

So, before starting to aim at relationships with individuals, it is crucial that you have a broad view of what your customers want, as a whole. It's no good starting with individuals if the bulk of your customers aren't happy and satisfied.

In other words, there are ascending levels of sophistication in marketing, with guesswork at the bottom, followed by general market research, leading on to the more targeted approaches aimed at building relationships with individuals.

We strongly recommend that you avoid guesswork, even though there are people who seem to get away with it, as you will see in Chapter 2. With the other two levels, it's a bit like learning to walk before you can run. So we're saying that your first steps should be to make sure your general market research is working properly before you go any further. You should already be using the basic information you need to run an effective organization, enabling you to provide goods and services that find a welcome niche in the wider market environment. Only then can you go further and build stronger, more personal relationships.

Let's look at this middle level of market research before moving on to the more sophisticated relationship level of the customer focus.

Using market research

Market research means looking at who your customers are – or who they could be – and identifying what they want from you, so that you can gear up the organization to meet their demands and requirements.

The results of market research can be used in a number of ways. At its simplest level, it can help organizations find out what their customers want, what they prefer and whether they are satisfied with the service they are receiving. As such, market research can be part of any customer-driven management initiative. It makes sense to investigate customers' reactions to the services which are available.

You can use market research to help you in all sorts of ways, including:

- develop performance indicators
- set standards
- develop new products and services
- start and grow businesses
- develop, maintain and increase market share
- monitor service quality
- develop a service charter.

This is how one market researcher sees the benefits of market research.

- It provides PR – the information gathered from market research can be published both internally and externally. This means the validity of the research must be good enough to stand up to close scrutiny
- It helps you develop your organization or department's strategy. Both qualitative and quantitative research can help you make plans and set strategy
- It allows you to check at regular intervals if you are on the right track
- It helps decision making.

Nick Winkfield, *British Public Opinion*

Yes ... but

'Yes, but', means 'No'. So never start market research unless you *really* want to know what you say you want to know. If you're thinking of doing it to try and get a nice warm glow from happy customers, forget it. Don't waste your time and money.

Real market research is a process that can be painful, embarrassing and difficult, because you want people to tell you the truth about your goods and services. It is going to be constructive and positive, but it might mean you hear about things that are not always what you'd hoped. *And that's what you're after.*

So, if you undertake market research and find that some people aren't happy with what you provide, avoid at all costs justifying your position by saying something like, 'Yes, but, you don't understand'. It's you that needs to understand ... to understand that they can leave you and go somewhere else for their goods and services at the drop of a hat. All the bluster and protests in the world won't make a dissatisfied customer feel any better; the chances are they'll feel resentful as well as let down if you start to imply they're mistaken.

The best tip here is always bear in mind a simple maxim you'll see repeated in this book.

If you aren't going to listen to the answers, don't ask the questions.

This is marketing

■ ■ ■

A standard definition of marketing is:

> **the management process of identifying, anticipating and satisfying customer requirements at a profit.**
>
> Chartered Institute of Marketing

So it's more than advertising, selling, promotion or research. It's the way you approach the whole business. It's more a philosophy than a series of quick fixes and research is just one crucial aspect of it.

In the definition, the verbs 'identifying' and 'anticipating' come before 'satisfying'. So it is in the process. It starts with basic market research.

There are lots of books devoted to a detailed look at 'formal' market research. This is not one of them. However, it is important to touch on the different aspects of market research and how each one can help you to understand your customers.

Market research describes a range of techniques aimed at getting to people's opinions, thoughts and preferences. These techniques range from sitting down and reading, through wide-scale statistically valid surveys to more informal discussions with individuals or groups. Whatever research action is being taken there are two questions you must keep at the front of your mind:

- what do I need to find out?
- how can I find it out?

What you need to find out

■ ■ ■

The very basic questions you want answered through research are:

- who are the customers, or potential customers?
- what do they require, precisely?

Only when you know the answers to these apparently simple questions – the 'identifying' and 'anticipating' parts of the definition above – can you start to work out how to satisfy customers.

Who are the customers?

This is very rarely as clear-cut as it might seem at first glance. Granted, a warship manufacturer has customers who tend to be fairly large and homogeneous – governments and their navies. But most people don't sell ships and most customers aren't that distinct.

For instance, who is the customer for baby food? Is it the baby or is it the parent? And what if you're a wholesaler who doesn't sell baby food direct to families but supplies local shops; who is your customer then? Or, what if you supply the person managing the child-care facilities at a holiday camp?

The same end user, or consumer, finishes up eating the food. It's designed to be eaten by a baby, after all. But one organization could be supplying:

- parents who buy on behalf of their offspring
- shopkeepers who sell it on to their customers
- organizations like holiday camps, childrens homes or hospitals, that buy it in for their little charges.

The key issue here is that none of these customers want the same benefits from the supplier. Naturally, the food has to be palatable or it won't get eaten, and it won't get bought. But take that as a given and you start to see major differences in the requirements of these customer groupings. Almost certainly, no single factor can meet the individual requirements of a range of market segments.

This approach is essentially market segmentation – different segments or customer groups have their own unique expectations from the products and services you supply.

What precisely do they expect?

Let's extend the simple example of the baby food.

Ask yourself, what does each of these groups want from baby food? You might come up with answers like these.

Parents: They certainly want the security of knowing that it is nutritious, safe, high quality and palatable. They have their own emotional need to feel confident that their child enjoys it and benefits from eating it. They want it at a sensible price, in a package that is big enough to satisfy baby's appetite but not so big that some ends up being thrown away. They want it easy to open and they want it available where they go shopping.

Shopkeeper: They want the manufacturer to provide advertising to promote sales. They want a good mark-up so they can make a profit. They want point-of-sale display material and attractive packaging to help sell stock. They want guaranteed deliveries in reasonably manageable amounts. They want new flavours and varieties introduced to keep the product selling. They want a representative to call in and make sure the merchandising is taken care of.

Institutions: They want keen bulk discounts and guaranteed delivery. They want extended credit to recognize the amount they buy. They want consistency of quality so they have no worries about what they are feeding youngsters. They want a brand name that reassures the parents of the children they are looking after. They want it to have a long shelf-life so they can cope with fluctuating demand.

You can see from this that there are several market segments, all buying baby food and all wanting something different from it. You can apply the same principles to everything from toilet tissue – eg domestic, hotel, public convenience and hospitals – to cars; fleet buyers, car hire firms and individual buyers.

You can also apply it to your organization. Think about it – hard. Who are your main customer groups and what exactly do they want? Think behind the obvious answer, and look for the reasons they buy it rather than what it is they buy.

Focus on solutions and benefits

Whether you make and sell products, provide services that the public pay for, or work in the public sector, the same core issue should be with you all the time. It is simple, powerful and not always easy to accept. You should be saying to yourself regularly and loudly:

> ***Customers buy solutions to their problems– not products or services. Without them I don't have a business or a job.***

Whether you sell cars or treat patients in the NHS, you depend on customers (even if they are called patients, clients or service users). No customers – no organization. And customers are more sophisticated than ever before, because there is more market choice than ever before. Every time a customer comes to you they want you to help them solve a problem, even if they don't define it for themselves in exactly that way.

Always focus on the fact that their expectations are about solutions to problems and not about product features. So factual descriptions like, 'It's four feet long and yellow', are meaningless because they don't relate directly to the problem. What helps them solve their problem is when you say, 'It does what you need *and* it's short enough to let you store it without any bother. Also, its colour means you'll never lose it'.

SPARKING OFF REPEAT BUSINESS

In a national survey on customer perceptions of electricians, the aim was to identify what led customers to value some individuals higher then others. In other words, why did they pick the electrician they did and why did they ask them back to do more work?

Many people looking for an electrician took a chance first time – they found advertisements they liked in the Yellow Pages. But a very high proportion used the recommendation of friends and family. These groups recommended people that they would use again, so the same sort of factors were common to why people chose someone, and why they asked them back.

▶

> And some fairly predictable factors came out – price, availability, good timekeeping and so on. But the fascinating thing was that the most commonly mentioned benefits of using certain electricians had absolutely nothing to do with whether they had City and Guilds certificates or were professionally qualified.
>
> The biggest factors were whether they cleaned up after them and vacuumed up all the dust and the mess, and whether they communicated in simple English about what was happening.

There are hundreds of competent electricians. What marks out the successful ones isn't whether they can handle a screwdriver. It's how well they came up with the solution to a problem the customer has in their mind, based on past experiences of other electricians. So, it appears that most people expect all electricians to be reasonably competent technically, but fear that they will be left with a mess after the electrician has left. That's the customer's problem. The fact that this electrician solves that apparently trivial problem makes all the difference. It's simple differentiation between the majority of suppliers and the one with that special something, that solves the problem.

Ask yourself, among the High Street banks, what differences are there in the range of services they offer? Virtually none. They all offer cheque books, business accounts, loans, mortgages etc. They all have branches, and holes in the wall where you can stick in a piece of plastic and get out cash. So what's the difference between them?

The answer is both simple to state and hard to quantify. It's the degree of benefit that individuals perceive their bank gives them over the others. It's not about basic services – they're virtually universal wherever you bank. It's about small and personal issues that make someone feel that their bank offers them more benefit than a competitor – like handy parking at the local branch, a manager who really listens, or cash dispensers that work.

We use the bank we do because it offers us as individuals more benefit than we would get from moving somewhere else, and that could come down to something as simple as where it is located. We don't choose it because it provides cheques. We choose it for the amount of benefit it gives us, in our daily lives.

So, when you thought about what your organization supplies to its customers you should have been thinking benefits. People don't buy products or services – they buy the benefits that the goods or services give them , and the peripheral experiences that go with the core product or service. These are what customers really require, and the issues on which they decide where to put their business next time.

Think about something you have bought in the past – say, a video recorder. Now think about why you bought the one you did. Was it because it was in a shiny black box, with the ability to record 76 channels, 28 years into the future? Or was it because it:

- allows you to watch one TV channel while not missing something on another
- lets you enjoy watching rented films without having to go to the cinema
- means you can keep up with neighbours and friends
- gives you the chance to watch your own holiday videos
- keeps the children quiet for the first two hours on a Saturday morning
- was exceptionally easy to programme and set up?

Whatever the reasons, they are about what the video does for you – what benefits it imparts to you – and not just what it is, technically. This concept of separating out benefits from technical features is central to professional selling in all its forms. It is absolutely crucial when you research what your customers require and expect.

Because of all this, it's not enough just to track numbers and statistics through market research. You can prove this to yourself by asking, if you have 1,000 customers and only 1 complaint, whether you are absolutely confident you have 999 satisfied customers.

MIXED BLESSINGS

An NHS Trust in the West Country introduced mixed sex wards. It made the administration a lot easier. They decided to run it as a pilot and base the final decision on how many people said they didn't like it.

Although referrals from local GPs were declining, they had no complaints after six months, so carried on in the belief the idea was a well-received success.

Because the decline in patient numbers was a worry in the free market NHS, they appointed a client care officer whose job was to go round and look for ways of improving the service. She found that over 80 per cent of the patients either disliked or hated mixed wards. They hadn't complained because they didn't think there was any point. Instead, they told their GPs who were starting to 'buy' bed space from other local Trusts instead, to take their patients.

So, you have identified your key market segments and know that your quest is to find out exactly what makes them excited and thrilled.

How do you find out the answers to your questions?

■ ■ ■

You know now what you should be doing. It's just a question of finding out, now. And that's market research.

If you ask a cross-section of the public what springs to mind when they hear the words 'market research', you'd almost certainly get answers about being stopped in the High Street by someone with a clipboard, or maybe a postal survey about some product or service they have used.

This can be because when the time comes to gather information about customers and their requirements, many organizations miss what's under their noses and go off to carry out surveys and questionnaire interviews. There's absolutely nothing wrong with this direct approach. Indeed, asking people for their own views and feelings is commonly the best way of getting real first-hand information. So one option is certainly to use techniques like surveys and direct research. These are referred to in many text books as field research – you research directly with the customers at first hand and you have to get out there to do it. We'll come back to this later.

But market research can start a lot closer to home than that. You can start at your desk.

Researching existing information

There is a load of valuable information lurking in files in the organization, and publications available from the library or other bodies. This is often known as desk research, for obvious reasons.

Just think about the wealth of information that your organization has available in its files and databases right now, collected for purposes other than market research. A few examples of where to concentrate are:

- product and service order patterns, showing for instance what products and services are most popular, or have annual cycles of demand, or are increasing or declining in popularity
- sales values, indicating where most income is generated, where the best margins occur and which products and services appear to be valued most highly by customers
- customer ordering patterns, giving you the chance to identify which sorts of firm order what products or use which services, in which quantities and how frequently
- enquiries for products or services that aren't stock items
- field reports from sales and other 'sharp-end' staff.

Another area you can use in-house is how to make positive use of complaints – a topic we'll cover in a lot more detail in Chapter 3.

Other published material is available from competitors, from bodies like Trade Associations, the DTI, Enterprise Agencies, or the Economic Development Teams that exist in virtually all local councils. It can tell you what population growth or decline to expect, how the economy is going, which firms and industries are going up or down … and all manner of other things that can help you focus on what customer trends are likely to affect your organization.

So, the message here is that you can make a really worthwhile start on market research without even leaving the building. It may take a few phone calls and it will certainly take some time and effort, but it pays off.

Even with a clear picture from existing material though, it may be necessary to get out there and talk to individuals. It's certainly the best way to get information from the horse's mouth. In the NHS Trust where they introduced mixed wards, part of their desk research was to monitor patient numbers. If they hadn't done that, they wouldn't have known clearly that there was a problem and they wouldn't have appointed a client care officer. So their desk research triggered the need for more personal research.

Field research

Desk research tends to focus on the quantity side of the equation – how many, what cost, how often and what percentage of growth in demand. Field research gives you the chance to get into real dialogue with customers about their feelings and opinions.

Increasingly, organizations commission market surveys from a national research body. Both the private and public sector are now using market research companies to help them learn more about their customers. In some ways opinion surveys have become a fetish among some organizations – especially in privatized industries.

There are two main types of field survey research: quantitative and qualitative. On the quantitative side it can help develop and test the findings of earlier desk research, and provide extra statistical information from which to identify trends. Field research on quantitative issues asks questions like, 'How often', 'How much', 'How many' and 'Which?'

Quantitative research works by asking a large number of people exactly the same questions about the same subjects. The resulting data from all these people allow you to show how many and what proportion of the sample members fall into different categories. (What proportion of people in the survey have a bank account for instance.) The aim is to produce statistically valid results. This is very useful stuff but it needs to be brought to life by having a qualitative element injected into the picture.

The quality issue

■ ■ ■

Qualitative research is not about finding out proportions or numbers. It is about asking the why question: why do people want to have one service rather than another, why would they rather do X than Y? Qualitative research aims to find out, in-depth, why people believe something. Instead of 'How many' it asks questions like 'What do you think of ...'.

An example of what qualitative research might be used for is people's attitudes and behaviour on environmental issues. Because the subject is complex, it would be difficult to draw out information with just a few preprepared rigid questions. Qualitative research helps us to understand people's motivations and responses.

The question is, how do we go about it?

Methods

Qualitative research is carried out using a range of methods, which include:

- face-to-face interviews
- taped interviews
- telephone interviews

- lengthy discussions
- postal questionnaires
- group discussions
- semi-structured surveys.

Do it yourself

You can do a lot of field research yourself, using very simple questions in any of the formats listed above. You can ask existing customers, for instance, so that you know what their real feelings and experiences are, and can develop service quality so it meets their requirements consistently. As a bonus, you can use that same information to form judgements about what matters to other potential customers, so you can go for new business in the knowledge that you have worked out what is likely to turn them on.

One very simple example is used by several organizations that use field research internally, at the interface between their own different sections and departments. They regularly ask each other three questions, none of which has any statistical basis at all. The questions are all open questions, which means they can't be answered with a straight 'yes' or 'no' and they all delve into quality of service. The questions are these:

1. What do we supply you with?
2. How well do we meet your requirements?
3. Where could we do better?

If you were to ask your customers these questions, remember you need to listen to the answers. If they criticize, don't get defensive and start trying to explain why the customer has misunderstood, or why you really didn't get it wrong at all. Take it seriously and use the information to build better processes and systems for the future.

Remember too, that the act of asking the questions has a very constructive benefit attached. It gives a customer a very positive feeling that you care enough to ask – as long as you listen properly to what they tell you.

Sometimes, though, you need a bigger survey or an external view of things.

Buying it in

There are a range of options for 'buying in' to this kind of research. You can buy a few questions on an omnibus survey (where other organizations are also taking part) or have your research tailored individually. Not surprisingly, the more you want done for you specifically, the costlier it gets.

Quantitative and qualitative are not mutually exclusive. In fact, they compliment each other, as the NHS Trust mentioned in the earlier example proved. Each has its own place and its own advantages and disadvantages.

Whether to research quantity or quality

■ ■ ■

It's horses for courses, really. It depends on what you want to find out. Qualitative research allows people to talk relatively freely. This can allow some surprising results, ideas and opinions to emerge. The rigidly structured questionnaire, on the other hand, cannot necessarily unlock these opinions because it sticks to a script. In the hands of an experienced facilitator, more flexible qualitative research can produce some very interesting results.

> *'For years, money was spent on subsidising theatre. (Following some qualitative research) it turned out that the reason people were going to theatres wasn't because they wanted to see actors on a stage. They were going for a night out ... for entertainment.*
>
> *That kind of understanding resulted in Cardiff City Council spending three million pounds on adding some new bars and a new staircase to their Civic Theatre. This money hardly touched the theatre productions...but it resulted in vastly increased and more regular audiences for the theatre and people having a much better time .'*
>
> Nick Pearson, Welsh Customer Council

One of the main advantages of qualitative research is that it can identify areas of concern which can then be explored more 'scientifically' in a large-scale survey.

It also allows you to reach hard-to-get-to-people or groups because they can be hand-picked. When the National Customer Council did research on what people with senile dementia and their carers wanted from social services, it used qualitative research. Small groups of sufferers and carers were identified by self-help and voluntary groups and social services departments. The National Customer Council then arranged home visits and semi-structured interviews to get an insight into the needs of a group rarely canvassed before.

Quantitative research, on the other hand, has the benefit that it is statistically accurate. Importantly, if carried out effectively, it can be repeated on a regular basis to measure trends and give organizations a benchmark to work against.

Commissioning market research

Many people have asked that we include a beginner's guide to commissioning primary market research, so the following should be helpful if you're in that position.

It is often assumed that commissioning market research is costly. It can be, but there are low-cost ways too.

This is an important point. Don't be put off from making even the most modest start because you think commissioning research must be expensive. Simply knocking on doors and asking twenty people what they think about your service doesn't cost much, and it's infinitely better than sitting behind a desk and guessing.

You can use a market research company or run the research yourself. We will look at some ideas for both. Whatever you decide on, it is important to make sure you know the answers to the following questions. They form the basic specification that either you or a firm you contract will work to.

1 Who are your customers?

Before commissioning research you must be clear who your customers are. This tends to be much less clear cut in the public sector than in the private sector. Think about market segments and target the appropriate groups. Sending a questionnaire to 24,000 households when you want to research how local greengrocers feel is clearly a waste of time and effort.

2 Why are you commissioning the research?

You must know precisely what you want to achieve and how you intend using the information before you start. Setting clear objectives not only makes the whole exercise more sharply focused, it means you can find out if there is someone else already carrying out similar research. If so, carrying out your own could lead to expensive duplication.

3 What resources do you have available?

Any research costs money and will tie up resources like time and people. You will need to weigh up carefully what resources you have available and match these to the different research methods.

4 What is your timetable?

Set realistic deadlines for when you need the information. It's no good doing market research about the millennium celebrations and getting the results three weeks before the end of the century. Again, this will affect the kind of research method you choose.

5 What methods do I use?

Now you've answered the four basic questions you can start the process of doing your market research. There are several possible methods in common use. While there aren't any hard and fast rules, in-depth interviews and discussion groups tend to work best where you want qualitative research, whereas for quantitative issues surveys and satisfaction monitors often fit the bill neatly.

Remember the resources issue, as well. Look at the potential benefits and the potential costs of different approaches and weigh them up. You may not be able to afford the full survey you'd like in an ideal world, but as long as your key objectives can be met there is always a choice and some scope for flexibility.

Have a look in more detail at how some of the common methods work.

In-depth interviews

In-depth interviews are usually carried out one to one by a skilled interviewer. The interviewer will have a topic guide rather than an interview schedule or questionnaire to guide them. A topic guide allows interviewers to get to the respondents' interests and perspectives on the issues. In-depth interviews are unlikely to be less than thirty minutes long.

The resources needed to run in-depth interviews are:

- an effectively designed topic guide
- a trained interviewer
- some way of transcribing the interviews
- the expertise rigorously to analyze the results.

A tape recorder, good microphone and a private room or other location for the interview will also be needed.

Small discussion groups

Between six and ten people is the ideal size for a discussion group. These people are led through a topic guide by a facilitator. The role of the facilitator is to keep the group focused but allow them to discuss the topic in the way they want. Discussion groups usually last between one and two hours.

The resources needed for a discussion group are:

- the physical resources – a room with adequate access, flip charts, refreshments, maybe transport etc.
- a group of people ready to make honest and open contributions; these people should have the same sort of characteristics as your typical customer

- a brief that is crystal clear
- a well-trained facilitator
- sometimes an observer and recorder
- someone sufficiently trained to carry out a later rigorous analysis (who may be the facilitator or observer, but may need to be someone else).

If you do it to the highest specification you might also need audio or video recording equipment and transcribing facilities. Consequently, if you commission a professional research company to carry out qualitative research in a discussion group it is unlikely to cost less than £5,000.

On the other hand, you can set up customer panels that are permanent or semi-permanent, as you'll see before this chapter ends.

Surveys

To carry out any survey, you need the following kind of resources:

- a good quality questionnaire which has been tested in the field and piloted to make sure that it is reliable
- a reliable sample of people (contacting them all may be costly)
- the personnel to carry out the interviews.

Also, don't forget the costs of collating and analyzing the data.

It is important to remember that you don't need to become a market research expert to commission market research. You may be able to get some free advice on sampling and asking unbiased questions from local college lecturers. If you commission a professional company, this advice will be part of the service.

Omnibus surveys

An omnibus survey is a survey which is regularly carried out by a major company in which anyone can buy one or more questions. The information from the questions is provided exclusively to the people that buy them. A good survey company will help and advise you to write suitable questions.

This can be a cheap way of surveying all people or a large proportion of people, for instance, council tenants. It is probably unsuitable if you want to target a more specific group like disabled people in a specific local authority.

The cost of buying one question on a reputable omnibus survey is around £450, which make this the cheapest type of market research. It is important to shop around for the best company for you.

Satisfaction monitors

There are a number available. National Opinion Polls, for instance, conduct a weekly monitor of public opinion in the public utilities and local and central government.

Commissioning market research companies

The key things about commissioning a market research company are getting the brief right and choosing the best company for your needs. Following the steps above should help you to get the right research method and brief.

There are many market research companies in the market and it can be hard to decide on the right one for you. Always get a number of quotations from different market research companies. Tender prices can vary by 100 per cent and it can be hard to choose between them.

Doing the research yourself

You may decide not to involve a market research company at all. If budgets are very tight but you do have access to people prepared to give up time, you may want to get volunteers to help run your own market research. However, if you decide to do your own research, always be realistic. Interviewing is a very difficult job, especially when it comes to the listening part. This is the part that most of the human race seems to find incredibly hard to do. We'd rather talk than listen. But listening is not just waiting for your turn to talk.

So people without interviewing skills will need support and supervision and will not produce the most reliable results. If volunteers start arguing with people they're interviewing it will do more harm than good. Think hard before tackling professional research methods using amateurs, unless your budget stretches to using professional interviewers, it is almost certainly better to keep your research project on a smaller scale and avoid any risk of problems arising from poor interviewing techniques.

If you can't use interviewers in any real depth, an alternative approach is to set up a customer panel or a focus group. This is something that can give you a detailed representative picture from a selection of customers, rather than gather an in-depth view from a very wide range. It's a method which you can use to test things like:

- products
- prices
- specific issues of concern.

Customer panels

■ ■ ■

Customer panels are not a new idea. British Telecom set its first panel up over ten years ago and still uses panels today.

What are customer panels?

A customer panel is a group of customers put together by companies to comment on, and make suggestions for, changes and improvements to the service.

A customer panel will meet regularly and will normally consist of the same members over a number of years. The number of people on these panels varies, but is usually no more than around twelve. The way panel members are selected also varies.

Some panels are made up of representatives from concerned organizations, others have actual service users.

The central purpose of all customer panels is to create an on-going dialogue between service providers with a group of specially selected people.

The advantages of customer panels

Customer panels have a number of advantages.

- Because panels meet regularly they can give feedback on current issues and events. This means they are highly adaptable. A panel meeting can tackle issues as they happen. Also, you can ask a panel member follow-up questions if you need to

- Panels, particularly local ones, can be relatively inexpensive to run
- Panels can open up access to managers at all levels in an organization: from junior managers to the chief executive. Panels act as a forum within which managers have direct, face-to-face access to customers
- Panel members either start out or become more 'expert' than a random sample of 'ordinary' customers. This means they can offer highly informed and valuable feedback
- Because customer panels use the same group of people over a period of time they can help build a climate of trust between managers and customers. Managers learn what motivates customers and customers gain insight into the constraints and choices faced by public sector managers.

An ideal customer panel

- Panels require carefully selected and effective members. These members need to be able to make an effective contribution and be independent enough to say what is on their minds, even if it is unpopular or controversial.

Closely allied with this is the need for the panel to be given an absolutely clear remit. Panel members also need to be clear about their role and responsibilities.

Effective panels will also need:

- somewhere convenient and accessible to meet
- an efficient secretariat to provide panel members with up-to-date information and administrative support
- training
- a budget for any travelling or accommodation
- a 'sell-by date' for members. This will keep panel members fresh and prevent panellists losing sight of the customer agenda
- a mechanizm to allow panel members to influence or set the panel's agenda
- access to mangers with the power to make changes – this will stop the panel simply being seen as a talking shop.

Although not essential, panels benefit from having an independent facilitator to chair meetings.

Case study

BRITISH TELECOM LIAISON PANELS

British Telecom (BT) has two types of customer panels:

- customer barometer panels
- special issues panels.

BT have two customer barometer panels – one in Wales and one in Scotland. Each is made up of around twelve panellists and can discuss any telecommunications issue.

BT put a lot of effort into recruiting panellists. They use external recruiters to do the job. BT's ideal panellist is a person who:

- reflects the geographical area
- can make a good contribution

▶

- is able to work with other panel members
- can enliven the working lives of BT managers.

Panel recruiters aim for a panel that covers a range of people of different ages, different backgrounds and different temperaments. They look for a mixture of men and women and for people from ethnic minority backgrounds. The vetting process includes face-to-face interviews. Each panellist has a two/three year 'sell-by date'.

BT sees its panels as 'not about convincing customers, but a forum where managers listen, consider, discuss and respond'.

Each panel is supported by a secretariat and attended by a customer services manger who can present panel ideas to the relevant people within the company. The ideas from the panel also form part of a six-monthly report to senior managers.

BT's specialist panels cover single issues. Members are drawn from wider geographical areas than the barometer panels and include some specialists.

BT's panels are backed up by a range of other consultative exercises.

The cost

BT give a very rough costing of around £25,000 per panel per year.

Lessons to learn

- BT took time to recruit panel members
- Panel members were given 'sell-by dates'
- BT use panels as part of a range of consultation activities
- BT use panels for both single issues and as more general forums
- Panellists are given access to managers who can take the ideas the panel generates and turn them into action.

Customer panels are an almost permanent feature in the listening war. In the next chapter we'll look at some other ways of building permanent 'listening posts' as an adjunct to one-off research.

The round up

■ ■ ■

This chapter has looked at some of the broad uses of market research. It comes towards the beginning of the book because it's a way of looking more broadly at segments and markets. However, it has looked at some detailed ideas and techniques you can use to get to understand customers more effectively. These include:

- consumer panels
- focus group
- questionnaires.

Market research is interesting because you can use it for a number of different purposes. It can be used both qualitatively and quantitatively, depending on what you want to get out of it.

The important thing with market research is that it gives you information, and when you have information about your customers, you can start taking sensible decisions about how you are going to fulfil their aspirations.

What's more market research doesn't need to cost you a fortune. It is something you can do right now.

However, it is worth bearing in mind that many of the traditional approaches to market research are being eroded. Simply using a snapshot approach and then targeting communications from you to customers does not start that all important dialogue going.

Later in the book in Chapters 5 to 7 we look in detail at how to develop a new approach to customers a million miles away from the traditional marketing approach.

2

How to be of the market

The historical context

Today's consumer market is crowded and highly competitive. All companies face the problem of how to stay in touch with customers.

Firms who make consumer products are launching more and more consumer products. In 1994, 20,076 new consumer goods appeared in America's supermarkets and drugstores. Consumers are faced with an avalanche of choice.

Obviously, most new products are tested before they are launched. Producers try to make sure that their goods meet the needs of their prospective customers. Getting to know customers is not just big business it is also a business imperative. But, given that so much money goes into it, how is it that no more than 10 per cent of new products are successful enough to be on the market two years after their launch? Launching new products is costly and so finding out what customers really want is doubly important.

This is the organizational and business dilemma just about all organizations face. You need to know what your customers want in order to deliver it, but how do you get to know reliably what they want and continue to want? OK – you can do the basic market research you looked at in Chapter 1, but everyone with any sense does that. What is happening in the business world that extends that familiar marketing view … is there a need to change views, opinions, beliefs and philosophy, as well as just practices?

The answer is a clear YES. That's what this book is about – helping you to stay in touch with customers and building a relationship with them over time, so you can keep them for life.

As such, the book plugs into a historical moment. In the 1980s and early 1990s the organizational emphasis was on creating powerful brands and mass markets with standard products to match. The phrase on the lips of the quality gurus of the time. The message then was 'the absolute need to iron out variance'. It fitted quite neatly with traditional views of customers and market research.

The late 90s is marching to a different beat. The emphasis is still on strong brands but it is now also on creating products and services that can be personalized to fit individuals and on developing on-going relationships with customers that create strong customer loyalty.

The methods organizations are using to develop this understanding relationship are almost as diverse as the companies themselves.

The following is just one example of how new technology is helping organizations to keep in touch with customers and, of course, to keep one step ahead of the competition.

USING DATABASE MARKETING

Organizations are increasingly using high-power computer databases to help them understand customers and target goods and services effectively. These computers have software which acts rather like the human brain. It can pick out trends among all the soft data and help companies speak directly to individuals. In a recent survey of large British businesses, almost half of those who replied said they saw database marketing as a major tool over the next five years.

A recent article in *The Economist* pointed out that the food division of US giant Philip Morris now has the addresses of 30 million customers who replied to free sample offers and promotions on its database.

Of course, in the UK, the airlines like British Airways and the banks like TSB have pioneered major customer databases that allow them to know a lot about their customers and use it to offer services and give customers a range of choices in areas they are likely to be interested in.

Proctor & Gamble uses its database to market the disposable nappies Pampers. The database generates 'individualized' birthday cards for babies and sends letters to parents reminding them to move their babies up to the next size nappy.

The programmes get ever more sophisticated and represent just one way of helping companies stay in touch and offering a more individual service.

This database marketing is just one approach. This book looks at a whole range – from the everyday and mundane to the high-tech; from the organizational to the things you can do as an individual right now.

Running right through this book is the belief that organizations of all types – be they public, private or voluntary sector – only succed if they:

- ***respect*** their customers
- take the time and trouble to ***find out what they think*** about the service
- find out what their customers' ***aspirations*** and wants are
- ***keep in touch*** with customers
- see them as ***individuals***
- keep them ***happy***.

At the heart of this, at all levels in a company, is the need to develop a team of people who see it as their job to keep in touch with customers and act as informal customer champions.

This book was originally going to be called *Learning to Love Your Customers* – and in many ways this title captured some of its essence.

The whole thrust is that in today's environment quality organizations take time to understand and respect customers and that they do everything to focus attention on them.

Big is beautiful

■ ■ ■

In the film *Big*, Tom Hanks plays an American schoolboy who goes to a fairground. He goes to get on a ride but is turned away because he's too small. A few moments later he comes across a mysterious wish machine complete with a Gypsy Rose Lee character stuck inside a glass case. He puts in his money, and makes his wish. He wishes ... *that I was bigger so I could get on the ride*. A small token comes out of the machine, saying his wish is granted. He wakes up the next morning to find he's in the body of a fully grown adult, but still with the childish mind and emotions he had the day before.

The story is an engaging, comic yarn about the way this mixture of age and childhood affects the character's life. He becomes a successful company executive in a toy firm – successful because he takes the child's eye view of what makes toys work, and has a clear advantage over his much more sophisticated and well-educated colleagues. In fact, he knocks the marketing team – with their MBAs and sophisticated computer packages and marketing-speak – into oblivion. Despite their fancy strategies they don't really understand what their customers want. The marketeers problem is that they make assumptions which they never think to really test out.

The Tom Hanks character, however, knows exactly what the market wants because he is of the market. He understands intimately and from the inside why children like certain toys, and uses this knowledge to steer the company and himself to great success.

Big is a parable about growing up, and it's also a film about the way corporations work. Above all, though, it is a film about learning to love your customers. The basic tenet of the film is that if you really understand what customers want, and stay in contact with their wishes, then you can't go wrong.

Obviously no-one would recommend the drastic measures taken by Tom Hanks. A country full of grown-up children running big companies probably wouldn't be a successful recipe for a growing economy.

However, the film is interesting because it does give us some insights into the way companies and marketing departments sometimes work and presents an alternative view which may actually be one of the touchstones of this book:

Be of the market.

The challenge for most of us is how to remain in touch with the market and for some sad souls it's how to get in touch for the first time.

Why is it so important to understand your customers?

■ ■ ■

This sounds almost a facile question, but is one well worth investigating. However, in some organizations the gulf between customers and staff has become so wide it is a question that seems almost threatening.

So, why is it so important to understand customers?

The following example shows just what a mess organizations can get in if they get it wrong.

'GOOD MORNING PURLEY'

Chris Tarrant is a TV presenter and breakfast show DJ for London's Capital Radio. His show is irreverent and grown-up. One morning he told listeners how he had just received a letter from his business bank manager at the High Street bank where he holds his account. No-one likes receiving letters from the bank, but this one was a Godsend for Tarrant. It went:

▶

> Dear Mr Tarrant
> I have pleasure in inviting you to a business breakfast at the branch. Food and drink will be served and you will get a chance to meet other business people from the local community and to talk to me. You are a valued customer. Please come along to the branch in Purley between 8.00 and 9.30 next Tuesday.
>
> Chris Tarrant commented thus:
>
> *'If I am such a valued customer you would have thought the guy would have taken the trouble to find out I am actually rather busy between 8.00 and 9.30 in the morning. On second thoughts though maybe I should skip work here, get up early and head on down to Purley High Street. And they probably charged me for the letter too!'*

Although slightly frivolous this example is at the heart of why it is so important to *really* know your customers.

For a start the computer generated letter showed quite obviously that the bank had no real knowledge of the customer. What's worse, is that it was the *business* side of the bank which had no knowledge of the *business* activity of one of their more important and high-profile customers.

The computer-generated letter only served to increase the feeling of the bank being out of touch. Their market research may have told them that people generally liked the personal touch and the invitation, but when the promotion came down to an important individual it fell flat on its face.

Importantly, what also contributed to the feeling of hamfistedness is the nature of the offer. Inviting someone to a clearly inappropriate business event simply makes the bank look stupid.

So the message is clear, organizations should only do this kind of thing if they do their research thoroughly and are serious about it. Indeed there are some very particular lessons to be gained from this relatively simple example.

An initial checklist

If you are serious about really getting to know your customers then:

- do your research thoroughly
- keep your information up-to-date
- don't use a scatter gun approach – aim at a target
- if you do use standard letters make sure they won't do more harm than good
- keep any communications with customers relevant – don't waste their time
- remember that customers are sophisticated receivers of information, they can spot junk mail a mile off and will know if you are not being sincere.

These should all be learned by heart.

The following gives a clear example of the consequences of not understanding your customers' aspirations. After all when people buy a service they are buying the experience and making an aspirational choice. If you show contempt for them or get out of touch with their aspirations then the consequences can be disastrous.

Could you come and do a speech, Mr Ratner?

■ ■ ■

A few years ago a successful businessman called Gerald Ratner stood up in front of an audience of some of his colleagues, at a business lunch in the City of London. He gave an engaging speech about his business methods. But he could have had no idea about the impact this speech would have. Just a few years later what was once a thriving chain of jewellers bearing the name of Ratner had plunged into debt, and Ratner himself had lost his position as head of the company.

These days, there isn't a Ratners in any High Street or mall anywhere in the world. The name has been written out of High

Street history – all because of one speech … one word. The word was 'crap'. Gerald Ratner described the goods customers bought from him as 'crap'. It was a throw-away joke intended to highlight that his business had successfully managed to bring what was previously a rather arcane and stuffy business – that of the High Street jewellers – within the reach of ordinary people. However, by calling his goods 'crap' his customers perceived him to be showing disdain for them. It sounded like he was laughing at them; conning them.

Anyone buying a piece of jewellery, however cheap, is buying emotional aspirations. Whether it's a wedding ring, a gift for a christening, a token on Mother's Day or a Christmas present the last thing anyone would do is knowingly buy crap. You want good value, sure, but you don't expect the Crown Jewels for a tenner, and no one sets out to buy crap. So saying that customers had bought rubbish when they had trusted Ratners to sell them decent presents came across as a direct insult to the people on whose goodwill a business is built.

Whether it was a slip of the tongue, just poor judgement or a real sneer at customers doesn't really matter now. The share value plummeted and people stopped going into Ratners.

Changing times

So, one of the first reasons for communicating with customers is simply the fast-changing nature of today's business world. If you don't keep in touch then you slip behind and they go elsewhere.

Take the banks as an example. In 1995 TSB launched its home banking service *Phonebank* as a direct result of its market research. The results told the bank that its customers wanted to bank from home. Phonebank has been a remarkable success for TSB. And many of the other High Street banks still have no homebanking. Where would you choose to put your account?

Another example here of how times are changing is the cinema industry. As out-of-town multiplexes spring up the in-town cinema faces strong competition. What's more, cinema-going is an aspirational thing and customers like the ease of parking and level of facilities of the multiplex. So how are the in-town cinemas to stay in the game? *The Independent* newspaper reports a novel strategy?

Indian films are being used by the MGM/Cannon chain as an opportunity to increase its cinema audiences, in a defensive strategy against the threat of out-of-town multiplexes.

Realizing they can't compete with some aspects of the multiplex the in-town cinemas have listened to what customers are asking for and plugged into a different market. The key to the strategy? Keeping in touch with the needs of the market.

Often keeping in touch is as much – if not more – about intuition as it is about expensive market research.

Some people in business seem to get away without market research. They simply *know* what their customers want. One theory here is that some people in some points of their lives are not so much looking in on a market – they are actually of it. Their tastes are our tastes and all they need to do is make or offer what they like and we will buy it in our droves. If they are very lucky these people may also shape our tastes too – so their tastes become our tastes.

If we think of people like this over the last twenty-five years then a number spring to mind. For instance:

- Sir Terence Conran – first with Habitat and now with his Conran empire of trendy shops and restaurants. Conran plugged into a desire for a more sophisticated home of a whole generation (few homes are without a touch of the Conran influence). And Conran's mission to put a decent salad bowl in the house of everyone in the UK.
- Anita Roddick – with her worldwide Body Shop idea. It is almost impossible to remember what it was like before Body Shop. Roddick captured and shaped and, to an extent, created our desire for green products and socially concerned shopping.

Often the companies who seem to instinctively understand the market are led by charismatic individuals. There is a danger here though. What happens when the market changes and you are no longer of it? Many UK business people have had five minutes of glory when they basked in the warm glow of leading fashion, only to end up out of touch and out of pocket.

Still, here are examples of people who simply knew what the market really wanted and were brave enough to follow their instincts.

THE SONY WALKMAN

When the initial idea for the Sony Walkman was suggested within the company it was greeted with a mixture of derision and scepticism. The view was that no one would want to carry around their music with them. However, the idea's originator stuck with it and the Walkman was introduced. The rest, of course, is history. It was a victory for intuition and for knowing what customers really wanted. And on the back of the technology the company grew still further.

THE GOLF GTI

When engineers at Volkswagen suggested there was a huge potential demand to be tapped if they hotted up the already successful hatchback for a new market niche, the management turned it down. There were no 'hot hatches' at the time and the idea of producing a small car that went really fast would never work, they said – that was an area that sports car makers covered.

Fortunately for Volkswagen, the engineers stuck at it, producing a prototype in their own time and wearing down the managers, and so succeeded in satisfying three million customers who bought one in the first two and a half years of production. The rest is history.

A word of caution though. For every Sony Walkman there are countless Sinclair C5s and other things that seemed a great idea at the time. Research and logic do play a part. It isn't all entrepreneurial mindreading.

Many businesses have made an effort to listen to their customers and to adapt and constantly look for improvements. They haven't traded on past glories or stuck to the notion that they know best and that they are doing the customer a favour with the service they are offering.

The rest of this book looks at the way you as a manager can help bring these principles of customer-focused business to bear in your department or within your team.

Finally, one more example. This is how a leading pub chain have gone about the business of reinventing their business based on what customers actually want. It is a remarkable story because it contains most of the elements we talk about throughout this book. It is a genuine study in how to learn to be close to your customers and how to keep close to them.

As you read through you will see that they:

- listened to customers intently
- listened to what staff had to say about what customers wanted
- made changes in the light of the findings
- kept in touch with customers over time to make sure what they were offering was still relevant
- saw a market opportunity based on their understanding of customers – both existing and potential – and took it
- broke taboos because of this knowledge. They decided not to go for the standard or traditional and instead to break the mould boldly
- saw one business day as in fact a series of different smaller markets made up of individuals with different aspirations
- worked hard to make customers feel part of the new entity and so saw repeat business as key to the success of the venture.

Case study

CREATING THE MODERN CUSTOMER-FOCUSED PUB

One of our leading pub chains decided that the British pub wasn't offering what its customers were looking for. All too often the traditional pub was a dingy, smoke-filled hole, catering for a certain type of man and alien to families, women on their own or business people.

The traditional pub

The traditional pub was fine if you wanted to go in and drink a skinful of Guinness, smoke and play darts or have a punch-up having chucked down ten pints of lager and some peanuts, while listening to an old tape of Deff Leppard selected by the barman. It wasn't fine if you wanted to go for a business lunch, or pop in with friends during the day, or take your children or go to listen to new music in the evening. Put simply, the British pub had become an anachronism, and wasn't flexible enough to cater for the many different markets that were out there. If you walk down to your local High Street the chances are you will find pubs like the ones above – although, of course, there have been changes.

As beer prices went up, the chain decided it needed to offer more to get people to come in.

So what did the chain do? Well, it started by listening to customers. It ran questionnaires asking what people wanted. It got staff to ask non-customers what put them off about coming into pubs and what they didn't like. The chain encouraged staff to visit other kinds of pub and bar and cafe to see what they were offering.

What they found out was that women often felt intimidated about going into pubs on their own. They found that business people didn't like going in at lunch time and being blasted out by music. They found that some of the more trendy youngsters regarded pubs as haunts for old people, and therefore wouldn't be seen dead in them. They'd rather spend their considerable disposable income in clubs. They also found that middle-aged people didn't want to go there because they felt frightened of possible violence. It seemed that the dear old British pub wasn't suiting anyone's needs.

So the company, using this feedback, invented the notion of eight pubs in a day. In other words, they would create the pub offering different things to different people at different times, reflecting the market segments.

One fine morning

Go into one of this chain's pubs in the morning and you'll find a perfect drop-in spot for people to visit with friends. Primarily aimed at women, this time-slot has an emphasis on light snacks, soft drinks and coffee. The music is designed to reflect a very laid-back mood. Staff are trained to be friendly to customers and use their skills to avoid women feeling intimidated by the pub atmosphere.

Time for lunch

Lunch time is when the business people come in. Staff get into smarter uniforms, the music changes and is much lighter. There is a range of food available, there are no smoking areas, and the whole tone is designed for people to feel free to take along business colleagues and prospective customers without the fear of being embarrassed.

As night falls ...

Early in the evening the pubs become family haunts. The music becomes more family-oriented, there is a family menu on offer, and staff who particularly like to work with children are specially selected for this period. After this early period there is time dedicated to middle income, middle aged people who want to come with their partners for a meal. Again, the menu, the music and the staff are tailored to reflect the market.

Through the rest of the night the pub becomes a kind of club. It plays modern and up-to-date music, offers designer drinks – often trendy 'designer' lagers – and it offers a very safe atmosphere with plenty of security, and a no-nonsense approach to any antisocial behaviour.

Slotting other market niches in between these main time slots allows the chain proudly to boast that the traditional English pub is no more. Instead they offer eight different pubs to eight different sets of customers, plugging directly into their wishes for how they want to spend their leisure time.

From the horse's mouth

As one of the directors said to us:

> *'People want to trade up in their leisure time. They don't want to go to dingy old smoke-filled holes which pubs used to be. We listened to what customers were telling us, and we have designed a product that fits exactly with it. What's more, we continue to listen, and are prepared to change this pub as much as is needed to keep in touch with what people want all the time.'*

Become obsessed with customers

You need to be obsessed with customers – obsessed about getting to know what they want and even more obsessed with the mission of delivering what they want. After all, it is the customer who pays your wages and who actually supports your whole organization.

No customers, no company ... it's as simple as that.

In an ideal world, this kind of customer obsession should take place across the whole organization. It should be built in to the marrow of the organization and be the backbone of the whole strategic planning process.

But even if it isn't a universal obsession, you can start the ball rolling. You, an individual manager, can enthuse your people to become more adept at listening to customers and start to feel comfortable with this kind of process. When others see the benefits that customer obsession brings, chances are they'll fall in with it enthusiastically ... even say they thought of it first, but who cares.

These are just four of the reasons why learning to love your customer is such a good idea.

Relationship not snapshot

If you get to know your customers you can build up a *relationship* with them over a long time. One of the things that has bedevilled British industry and organizations is the kind of 'snapshot' approach to customers. It's OK to get customers through the door once, but the real key is to get them to come back time and time again, and then start recommending you to their friends.

There is a saying in some successful selling quarters, that people buy from their friends. Think about it. When you go out to buy something, you may never have seen the sales assistant before in your life and what turns you off is a pushy assistant who tries to sell you something. What turns you on is the individual who becomes your friend by the end of the transaction – genuinely listening to you, caring about your needs and building up trust. So by the time you leave you feel you made a good purchase ... with the help of that nice sales assistant.

And you go back there ... they've got a customer for life. It is for this reason that many companies are increasingly shifting away from spending vast sums on advertising and switching the money to so-called *below the line activities*. For instance the £2 million advertising budget could be more profitably used to establish a loyalty scheme or to develop a database.

So learning to love your customers is a way of getting them to come back time and time again because you are consistently able to offer what they are looking for, and because they feel that your business means something to them.

One of the directors of the pub chain above explained why the initiative had worked so well:

> *'Every customer that comes in feels that the pub is theirs. They feel we have made it specifically for them and this brings great customer loyalty.'*

Loyalty cuts both ways.

Some organizations are working on cementing the relationship because it makes good sense. They have pledged a level of service or loyaly to customers. An example of this is that some companies have developed customer charters and service level agreements.

Others have developed customer promises. '*We will always answer the phone within three rings*' for instance.

These companies have made a statement that they intend to develop a longer-term relationship and that they have obligations as part of this.

Tailor-made services

When you have got to know what your customers want you can then start tailoring your product and services to them.

Old fashioned customer service values – encapsulated in the age-old maxim, the customer is always right – were overtaken by the marketing trends of post-war business. But the wheel is turning full circle. In many ways the notion of tailoring harks back to pre-20th century ways of doing business. Maybe the model for much of this thinking could be the old Edwardian department store – with its emphasis on service and choice of products. And of course on staff who knew their customers well and just what their tastes were.

This is certainly a useful antidote to our obsession with throwing standard products at mass markets and ironing out variance. You may be able to buy a McDonalds hamburger that is served and tastes the same from St Petersburg to Washington and back, but what about choice and variety? This is what Burger King have pushed to differentiate themselves from their competitors – you can mix and match at Burger King and the company's slogan is: 'YOU GOT IT.'

In a world where everyone insists on seeing themselves as an individual and absolutely unique, learning to love your customer can help you to start offering something individual to them. Ideas currently surfacing are, to say the least, weird and wonderful. There has been a suggestion for instance that we may soon be able to buy interactive films with a range of plots and endings to suit our tastes. There has even been a suggestion that alternative endings could be put together from out-takes of classic films. So everyone who always wanted Ingrid Bergman to stay with Humphrey Boghart may one day see their wishes come true.

Even local authorities are seeing the benefits of this way of looking at customers. For instance some now offer their tenants vouchers and a menu of options for repair and refurbishment. So, they can choose up to the level of their vouchers whether to have double glazing, or central heating and so on. This acknowledges that we are individuals and any service provider should tailor services to suit.

A HISTORICAL PERSPECTIVE

In the old days before mass markets and world-wide brands, traders pretty well knew what their customers were looking for, and would then develop products for them. For instance the old village baker may well bake a range of different breads for different people, all based on the same basic recipe. He or she would know intimately what they wanted and would then be able to deliver it to them.

One of the challenges facing today's organizations is whether it is possible to start offering a more tailored and personalized service based on understanding customers more fully. And the question arises – can big impersonal organizations remodel themselves to seem like small friendly businesses to customers?

The following is a true story.

THE PUBLISHING INDUSTRY

When I first started working in educational publishing we used to develop a whole range of generic products. There were courses on all kinds of things from wine making to management to accountancy. We were very good at generating new products but were probably not very good at knowing what our audience wanted. We handed them over to the sales people, crossed our fingers, and then got on with generating a new set of products.

The products we generated were not what one might call bespoke. They were designed for any person. But the problem with this 'any person' approach was that we didn't really have a clear idea of the market, and what they wanted, in our minds.

These days the same organization develops virtually no generic courses. What it does is use the courses we developed over three years and then adapt them to each individual customer's needs. This means that the old job of the commissioning editor generating lots of new courses is virtually dead and buried. The commissioning editor instead is a kind of consultant going in with a portfolio of existing materials and then working with the client to develop new ones that actually fit their needs.

This kind of approach has spread well beyond the bounds of just publishing.

44 Make or buy

There is a simple truth in effective management, that it is sometimes easier to make things than buy them.

With customers this means it is much easier and more productive if you can hang on to the customers you already have rather than keep having to get new ones to keep the business going. Keep the original customers and the new ones tend to just turn up, maybe with a bit of promotional encouragement.

The following is based on a small business.

THE SMALL BUSINESS DILEMMA

Small businesses frequently face the dilemma of how long to give to finding new business and how long to devote to doing the work they have.

All too often, they get the balance wrong. They either launch headlong into work, don't look for new business and end up when the work is finished with a difficult period where they desperately have to look for work. Or they spend so much time looking for new business that their existing customers suffer with missed deadlines and low quality work.

So, it's much better to keep on this longer term relationship with customers based on knowledge and respect, rather than consistently having to develop new customers and looking for them.

In increasingly competitive markets the act of finding new business all the time can be very expensive, and that doesn't mean expensive in terms of a big BT or Mercury bill. There is the back-up, the administration and the simple wear and tear on individuals brought about by consistently having to find new customers. There is also the bad will caused by the inevitable defections and complaints that come from high-customer turnover.

So, if you can, the key is to try to hang on to customers and develop more of a partnership relationship with them, based on knowledge rather than having to guess what new customers want.

ONE, TWO, THREE

Most airlines have massive customer databases, not for number-crunching but for relationship marketing. They generally categorize them as five star, four star and three star, or gold, silver and bronze, or some other such grouping. Anyone who books a seat on a plane is logged in the database – what food they like, whether they prefer a window seat, any special requirements and so on – so that when they book again the airline says they know them. 'Presumably you're still a vegetarian, Mr Jackson?'

Just think about the impact a relationship like this has on the loyalty of a passenger who has huge choice in which airline to pick. After all, they all fly to the same places, at roughly the same price, so as long as the service quality is consistent, the loyalty factor and the relationship are the only competitive edges available.

And on the front line

And of course there are real advantages to this approach especially on the front line.

In organizations that have got out of touch with customers there are often lots of complaints and friction between customers and front-line staff.

The list of problems that can arise include:

- a sense of alienation felt by customers towards the organization
- out-and-out conflict between customers and staff
- low motivation from staff – who wants to work in an organization whose customers hate it?
- a feeling of them and us between customers and staff
- actual disdain for customers
- violence towards staff.

The following example shows how getting in contact with customers can start to tackle some of these problems.

LEICESTER CITY COUNCIL

In 1987, Leicester City Council decided that it needed to get more in contact with local people. The catalyst for this was the level of confrontations taking place between front-line staff and local people.

On one memorable occasion a council member queuing up to pay his rates heard a customer reeling off a long list of reasons why the council was useless and why she shouldn't pay her rates. After the tirade the front-liner wearily added a colourful list of her own.

The council decided something had to change. They started by drawing up a formal complaints system so local people could make their views known rather than simply taking it out on staff on the front line.

The policy officer who steered the whole thing through said:

> *'We needed to get out from behind our desks and find out what our customers wanted or, in fact, didn't want. Complaints were part of a set of initiatives designed to help us to get closer to the public.'*

And of course to take some of the heat out of the contact between staff and customers. As another policy officer said:

'I was recently talking to front-line staff in the housing benefits office. They deal with over 1,000 people a week. It is a very high pressure job indeed. The staff who I spoke to said that they feel much more positive about picking up the phone and trying to sort out people's problems. By establishing a complaints system to listen to people it has shown staff that there can be satisfaction in even the most dire situations.'

Who are these people?

You have touched on why it is so important to actually listen to customers and find out what they are looking for from the service ... and you'll see a lot more later. But it's equally important at this early stage to get a clear picture of who your customers are.

All too often managers and organizations take a very narrow view of what makes a customer. Sure, the customer is the person who comes through the door and uses the service, paying for it either directly or indirectly.

But if you start to look more broadly you can see a whole range of customers, and other stakeholders, who are also worth listening to and understanding.

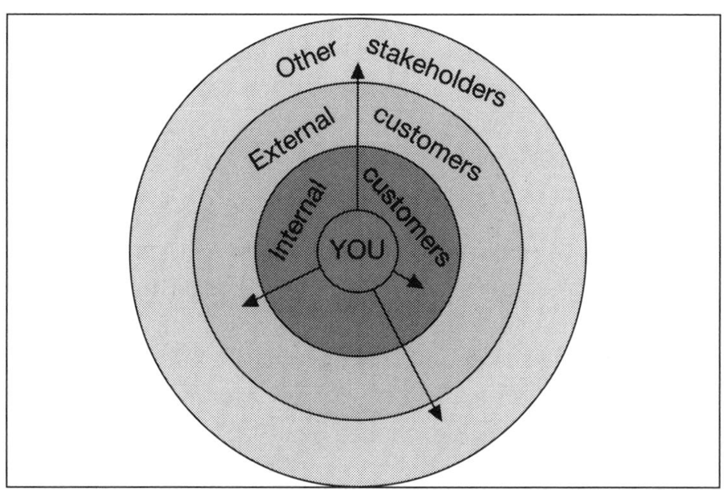

If you see yourself as the centre of things, and assume that everyone else is receiving something you send their way, they're all customers.

The external customers

These are the people who come through the door to use your service, who buy your product or who are your tenants, or whatever. They are the basic reason your organization exists.

It is pretty straightforward putting together a list of these customers and appreciating their importance. But what about colleagues at work? How important are they – to you and the external customer? The bottom line is that external customers generally rely on a range of people working together to meet their requirements. This means everyone inside the organization making sure they provide their colleagues with the right information, materials and goods to do their part of the work to standard.

The internal customers

Internal customers are like a chain. Everyone you hand on work or information to is your customer. You supply them with something they need and it has to be of the right quality or they can't get it right for the external customer. Any chain is as strong as its weakest link.

Your manager is your customer – you hand work and information on to your manager. So naturally you take the time to listen to what your manager has to say about you and what they require from you.

Other departments are customers. A key work relationship is between departments and if it breaks down it can cause many problems for you and your team, as well as the other department. If you become committed to listening to your customers then these people too should play a part in your considerations. The trouble is that there's often rivalry and even active warfare between departments that should be on the same side. Take the following example.

THOSE BLASTED SALES FOLK

'Where we work there is always a big demand between us and the sales department. We used to see them as meddling. They would come round, get in our way when we were trying to get on with our job. In fact there was quite a lot of tension between us. One day our manager decided it had to stop as it wasn't productive and it caused a lot of stress.

We then set upon a process of just trying to find out what it was that wasn't working properly. We ran seminars to explain the work that we did. We also had a secondment of one of the salespeople into our department, and one of our people went to work in Sales. It was amazing. We found out that while we should have been working together, we were in fact working against each other.

We now have regular briefing sessions and meetings. We work as one team across the organization rather than working against each other, but the important thing was that we stepped into each others shoes to see what it was that we were trying to achieve, and what got in our way.'

Other stakeholders

The people living near a factory have a stake in things, the staff do, so do your suppliers. Anyone with any interest, financial, environmental or otherwise is a stakeholder. So, for instance, suppliers are a major stakeholder in your business, whose comments about the organization they're supplying get ignored. But take the time and listen to suppliers and you may well find out some very interesting things that can make everyone's life a lot easier.

In the public sector the range of stakeholders can be frightening but ignore them at your peril.

Something to do

Write down all the different customers you have at work. When you have done that, think about how you would describe your relationship with them, and how much do you really know about what they want from the service that you provide?

The answers you gave are likely to be very different, depending on your different circumstances. However, this activity should have helped you start thinking about the different customers you have.

Doing a customer audit

One way that a company sometimes kicks off the process of learning to love their customers and focus on them is to pick out a number of key customers and ask them what they think about the service.

Some companies, for instance, have drawn up a list of their 50 top customers and then invited them either in to the company, or gone out to visit them to actually find out what they think.

This business of actually establishing who your key customers are is important so an early thing you can do is to carry out a customer audit that looks at who your customers are and who your most important customers are.

The first stage of any customer audit is to ask yourself some basic questions about your customers – on the lines of the basic market research on segmentation you looked at in the last chapter. These will help you get a rough kind of road map to help you be clear about where your customers are coming from.

So the kind of basic questions you might ask about your customers are:

- What is their age?
- What is their gender?
- What is their race?

When you have asked these questions you can start seeing whether there are any gaps. You may well see from this initial questioning that there are whole areas of the population that you as yet aren't getting to. When you ask these basic questions you can also ask another very basic question – what do I actually do for these customers? This will allow you again to start thinking about where your service fits in.

In his book *The Power of Relationship Marketing*, Tony Cram, gives the following example.

'A MARS A DAY'

Imagine you are running a small confectioners shop and two people come in, one after the other, and each buy a Mars bar.

Who is the most important customer? After all, they both bought a Mars bar.

Well, it turns out that the first person is an American student just passing through who is never likely to darken your door again.

The second is a person who walks every day past your shop with his dog, and it's the first time he has come in.

This means that this second customer could be very important to you if he buys a Mars bar from you every day for the next few years. After all, these small transactions all add up.

This is just one very simple example but it shows it pays to think through who are your really important customers, and then set up a mechanizm or some kind of way of constantly keeping in touch with what they actually like and what they want from your service.

Other questions you need to ask to get a real feeling for who are these key customers are things like:

- Who uses the service most frequently?
- Who spends the most?
- Who has the most influence in the terms of being an opinion former?
- Who is likely to have the most potential as a customer in the future?

Answer all these questions and you are likely to be able to help yourself start to develop a map of who your key customers are, although of course you shouldn't start neglecting the others. The point is that if you are starting from a low base you don't want to collect too much information. Instead, you want to start collecting information that will help you from the people that matter most at this moment.

Choosing representatives

If it is hard to pick out important customers you might simply pick representative ones who will give you useful feedback.

BT LIAISON PANEL

BT have set up a series of customer liaison panels. The customers on these are selected because they are typical of BT's customers – one might be a single young mum, another a business person. BT then gives these panels a free hand to debate areas they are concerned about. It also suggests areas that might be useful – like service standards. BT managers sit in and act as the panel secretariat.

And now, relationship marketing

■ ■ ■

You have looked a lot in this first chapter at why it is so important to learn to love your customers.

Many of the ideas connected with this book are often grouped under the umbrella of what is known as *relationship marketing*. You won't hear this phrase used much in this book because it is rather clumsy and smacks of marketing jargon. But it is worth touching on some of the ideas often expressed as the relationship marketing ethos because our approach and that of the proponents of relationship marketing do have much in common.

Relationship marketing is based on the idea that the most successful companies build up a longer-term relationship with customers. This approach relies on finding out what they want and trying to build as much of a one-to-one communication as possible.

So, companies that use relationship marketing will often set up databases to allow them to store lots of information about people's buying preferences and lifestyles which they can then use to tailor services and promotions towards them.

However, relationship marketing isn't just about databases and computers. In fact the basic ideas behind it are simple.

Think of a relationship you have. As part of this relationship you probably do the following things with the person:

- talk to them
- listen to them
- write to them
- phone them
- ask them what they like and don't like
- try to please them
- keep up to date with where they are – what they want to do, what they aspire to and what downright annoys them
- stay interested in them
- observe them
- treat them as an individual
- change your behaviour in response to theirs.

Relationship marketing stresses that companies should be doing all these things with customers.

And finally a reality check

■ ■ ■

It is important to be aware that when you start the process of getting closer to your customers you need to be aware of the *range* of things they are looking for from your service or product.

Often the range of things they take into account can be surprising. And certainly, price is only a component in their decison making.

Unless you are clear about the factors your customers take into account in choosing a product or service then it is hard to get to know them better.

The final part of this section will just present a few thoughts about what customers are looking for.

The truth is that customers will be looking for different things from a particular product or service – and sometimes their wishes can be complicated and even emotional. Their decisons are often tied up with their aspirations and beliefs.

So, when you get to ask them about that product or service you need to be aware of these different things that customers have in their minds, and the way they make decisions about whether to use you or one of your competitors. You look later at how to carry out an informal benchmarking exercise.

These are just some of the considerations that customers think about when they make a decision about whether to buy your product or service, or whether they decide to go to a competitor.

Price

Clearly price is important, but not the most important factor with many products and services. Do you always buy the cheapest? No, neither do the vast majority of people. Customers often have an idea about the price range in which they are prepared to buy a certain product. This can be complex, and tied up with all sorts of tangible and intangible things about value. However, for most products there is a band of pricing that people are prepared to tolerate, so when you are thinking about finding out what your customers want you need to be aware of where your product or service fits.

Remember, though, that price often comes low down on people's priority list.

Aspirations

When you buy a product or a service it's all tied up with your aspirations. If you are buying a Rolex watch or a Range Rover you are clearly trying to make a statement about yourself and your position. Even with small items this may be true. For instance shopping at Marks & Spencer reflects a certain aspirational quality.

Certainly, anyone whose offspring have insisted on one sweatshirt or one pair of trainers with the right name on them – costing three times the amount of what look like exactly the same or better – will understand. So you need to be clear in your mind about how aspirational your customers see your product. If they are looking to trade up with it, clearly this will have an impact on what they think about you and the product. So you need to be aware about where your product fits.

Reliability

Your product or service needs to be reliable. This is one of the markers that people have about anything. It's no good having a wonderful service experience on a British Rail train if it then turns up an hour late or breaks down one mile short of the station. You pay basically for reliability, the sure knowledge you'll get to your meeting on time. All the rest of it is frills. The fried breakfast was great, the executive magazine you got was good, even the copy of *The Daily Telegraph* had its uses. But what you really paid for was getting there on time. So reliability comes top of most lists of the things to get right. When you ask customers what they want this is likely to be a key marker.

Quality

Customers consistently make decisions about whether to buy goods or services based on quality. It's important to be clear about what we mean by quality because the word has a number of different meanings, or at least it has developed different meanings, some of which aren't quite accurate.

People often confuse quality with grade. In other words, both a Mini and a Rolls Royce are quality products. However, they are different grades. When people decide to buy goods or services, they take into account much more than simply the price. They decide whether it will fit in with their lifestyle, what experience they want, and whether it will make a statement about themselves that they are happy with. So when people make decisions about business services they are often basing these on quality.

A quality good or service is one that:

- is fit for the purpose
- does the job people want it to
- matches up with their expectations.

The round up

So in this chapter we have looked at a number of important ideas that will stay with us throughout the rest of this book. These are that:

- Big companies are increasingly attempting to take on the service standards and personal contacts of small companies
- There are many good reasons for getting closer to customers and staying close. These include the ability to hang on to customers for longer, and to stave off the competition
- Successful companies often develop a relationship with customers that goes beyond simply buying a product. They show a commitment to customers and a respect, and this in turn is rewarded with loyalty
- Effective companies develop an obsession with customers and this is shot through all layers of a company.

3

Make and take the time to listen

Stop

It sounds obvious, but before you try and listen to your customers, you need to stop and get ready. Give yourself the time to take these activities seriously.

There is a serious problem in management circles that you might need to overcome. It is about being seen to be busy. It shows up when managers don't feel they are doing anything unless they are dashing about sorting out crises, are under immense time pressures or are solving other people's problems.

You may recognize the feeling that leads to this. Imagine the boss walks in on you when you're thinking. You're not on the phone, or in a meeting, or even reading a report. You're just thinking ... gazing into space. For most individuals this feels like being caught out – as if there's some criminal act associated with thinking. A stream of excuses and apologies comes out to explain why you weren't 'doing anything'.

Forget it. You were doing something, something that gets done far too infrequently as a planned management activity. You were thinking. Celebrate the fact, recognize that if you don't spend quality time thinking you are likely to get moving in the wrong direction.

In the business of getting closer to customers, the first thing to think about is the art of listening.

Why listen?

■ ■ ■

Organizations who don't listen to their customers lose their customers – unless, of course they are a monopoly, in which case they get disaffected and unhappy customers.

The organizational world is awash with examples of companies who haven't listened, with disastrous results.

Take the followiong example. It shows how a big company didn't listen to customers and how those same previously loyal customers took against the company. Clearly listening to customers is one of the first ways of establishing a relationship that lasts.

Case study

NEW COKE

A few years ago Coca Cola in the USA decided that they had to make some changes. They were spending more than $100 million dollars more than Pepsi on advertising and yet they were losing market share. They decided to replace the existing product with New Coke and launch it as a replacement product. They carried out testings of the new product taste and found that people liked it, so they moved ahead.

But they admit now that they failed to ask a fairly fundamental question, 'How will people feel if the old product isn't available any more?' Mind you, Coke is just a soft drink so it's not really a question of feelings or emotions, is it? Well, yes, as it turned out. The whole story is about emotions and tradition, rather than the taste of a soft drink.

Within three days of the switch to New Coke, the company was receiving 8,000 calls of complaint a day. Acquaintances and passers-by in supermarkets and on the street abused Coca Cola executives, and some were even threatened with death. There were letters saying things like:

'You have personally stolen something from me ... it's mine and I want it back.'

'You have betrayed me and the American way of life.'

A black market trade started, with franchised bottling plants making and selling 'bootleg' old coke at three times the price. Illegal imports of the old product came in from Mexico and other countries. Coke trucks containing the old product were hijacked and the contents sold. Frank Olsen and Gary Milkins, in Seattle, started an organization called *The Old Cola Drinkers of America*. They set up a full time office and became hugely popular guests on TV talk shows. They said 'It's *my* drink ... it's part of our country'. They even went as far as suing Coca Cola in an unsuccessful attempt to get the old product reinstated.

For most of this time, Coca Cola executives seemed to be shutting their eyes and ears to the outcry. They didn't quite know what to do, but to the outside world it felt as if the company was doing what it wanted to do rather than listen to the customers. But they also had to take account of the fact that thousands of people apparently did like New Coke. They weren't saying much, but they were buying the product.

Something had to be done, clearly. The choices were to revert to the original position, stick to the new one or find some sort of middle way. Eventually, the Chief Executive announced they were responding to public pressure. Original Coca Cola was reborn as Classic Coke.

The whole experience took everyone by surprise.

What do we mean by listening?

■ ■ ■

Listening is an active two-way process. It is certainly at the heart of any relationship. Listening is certainly more than just hearing. It is an active process of assimilation.

This is all well and good, but how can managers go about listening to customers? Well, there are in fact a range of ways – from the immediate and simple through to the more complex and long term. What's more, innovative companies are consistently finding new and more effective ways to listen.

It is certainly true that listening to customers takes:

- concentration
- facilitation – you need to actively make and help it to happen and you may need to put a formal system in place.

Committing yourself to being a listening organization and/or team may also expose you to a degree of risk.

Learning to listen means letting customers set their own agenda. It also means finding ways of getting the views of those members of the community who may be harder to get at – people from ethnic minorities and people with disabilities for instance. Effective complaints systems, customer representative groups and some forms of market research can all be effective ways of reaching these target groups.

Some ways of listening

So listening is the royal road to knowing your customers.

The following are just some of the techniques you can use to listen to customers in order to understand them:

- undertaking some simple market research
- helping people develop an informal listening culture and the skills to support it
- establishing a formal feedback and complaints system.

We looked at the bones of market research in Chapter 2, so the other options are in focus here.

Developing a listening culture

■ ■ ■

It's not easy to forget this, but most managers have access to customers whenever they want. They meet them day in and day out. And it's through this business of coming into contact with customers that you can actually start finding out some very useful things about what they want. It is important though to bring listening into the culture of your team and organization. It needs to become second-nature.

The easiest way to start listening is to start easy. Put simply, all managers have the richest source of customer information at their fingertips – the customers themselves.

Try to answer the following questions.

As easy as 1, 2, 3

When was the last time you asked a customer what they thought of your service?

When was the last time you handled a customer complaint personally?

When was the last time one of your staff asked a customer about the service or products you provide?

If you answered, *within the last week*, then the chances are you are staying in contact with customers. If you answered in terms of months then you may be drifting dangerously out of touch.

We hasten to add that when we say asked a customer about the service we don't mean the following.

'EVERYTHING ALRIGHT MATE?'

'I was having an informal meeting with the director of a nationwide chain of hotels in one of the company's hotel lounges. We ordered coffee from the waiter. When nothing arrived we ordered it again and it arrived without an apology.

▶

About three weeks later, I met the same director in the same hotel. We had the same waiter. This time someone had clearly told him he should ask the customers if everything was alright. He appeared with a strangest looking lop-sided and twisted grin, that was clearly hurting his facial muscles to keep going. He served us, disappeared briefly and then, just as we were putting the cups to our mouths, he walked up silently behind us and bellowed out: "Everything alright mate?"

We couldn't reply within the five or six nano-seconds he waited, because it's hard to frame a sensible response with scalding coffee down your clothes and in your briefcase. So he shot off as quickly as he had arrived, clearly content that silence meant there was no problem.

I don't think this was quite what the waiter's managers meant when they told him they wanted him to listen to customers.'

There are a number of things you can do at once to start breaking down barriers between your staff and your customers.

Step 1

Explain to your people why you think it is important to get out and listen to customers and what you intend to do with the kind of information you receive.

Step 2

Lead by example. Make a point of being seen to talk to a customer at least once a day. Also show that you do care what customers think. You can use this to help your team take on your values as their own.

'I am a director of a housing trust. When tenants ring in with a problem I make a point of speaking to them. The tenanats are amazed because they don't expect to get through to the director. I see it as our duty to listen to our tenants. I also see it as free market research.

Last week I asked my secretary if anyone had called while I was out. She said: "No, only a resident."

I was furious. We spoke and I explained that the residents were why we all had a job and that we were there to listen and learn.'

Step 3

Encourage staff to get away from their desks and meet the customers as regularly as possible.

Step 4

Show that you do something with the results. There's no point listening if you don't act. So, when you learn something interesting try to make a change based on it and tell everyone what you have done.

Remember: listening informally is all free market research!

The following is a good example.

'WE DON'T LIKE THE MUSIC'

One day the manager in a large store received a complaint from a customer that the background music 'was absolutely horrible'.

Rather than act on just one complaint and change things instantly, the manager stopped and thought. Then she headed down to the busiest part of the store and asked fifty customers what they liked and didn't like about the music, what music they would prefer and so on.

The results revealed that the complainant was in a very small minority. Most people really liked the present music. Had they come out against it the manager would have suggested a change, but to change because one person shouted loudly when nobody else said anything would have been a mistake.

And what do you get as a result of encouraging this listening approach? Well, for a start you get a route into understanding a little about your customers. You don't exactly get an on-going relationship with customers but you do get some contact and the first bricks that will finally make a bridge.

One positive thing you will find, is that you get more positive than negative comments in many situations. Most people don't say thank you for good service, while some write in and condemn you for failures. Asking people opens up the contented end of the market and gives you a good, balanced view.

Learning to listen

With a start made on opening up a listening culture, it's time to work on listening skills. These are some of the hardest skills to develop and are certainly some of the most useful.

Try talking to a party bore. Well, maybe not, because you'll soon realize that there's no point. And the reason there is no point is that it is all one-way traffic. They do all the talking, you do all the listening. When you try to get a word in they either interrupt or don't listen and then they use your words as a neat springboard for talking about themselves again.

Years ago, in his classic book *How to Win Friends and Influence People**, Dale Carnegie said that if you want to give someone a clear and unshakeable impression that you're a brilliant conversationalist, learn to nod. His message was that if you say nothing, but just smile, nod and utter the occasional 'I see' or 'That's interesting', they'll go away absolutely convinced they've met the most interesting and interested conversationalist they've come across for ages. And you've said virtually nothing!

What they may not realize, of course, is that by listening you also now know an immense amount about what they value, what they want and what makes them tick.

Many managers – and the organizations they work for – miss

*World's Work Limited, 1953.

these points entirely. They do all the talking and the other person is simply on the receiving end of it. The saying goes, 'Telling is not selling', but they will insist on telling other people:

'this is what you want'
'this is what you need'
'I know what's best for you'
'I saw someone yesterday ... exactly the same as you.'

There's no one exactly the same as you or your organization. But even if there were, the last thing anyone wants to hear is that they're not special.

> *'If a business consultant really wants to turn me off, they only have to say they know what my company needs, because they solved exactly the same problem for someone else last month. My business is unique and I expect them to listen to my unique problems and come up with unique solutions.'*
>
> Chairperson of a Training and Enterprise Council, addressing a group of consultants

Managers and organizations make this basic mistake with little real knowledge or understanding of real customers in real situations. They develop a kind of composite or virtual reality customer, that they use as a base for all their decisions on services or products. Far better, surely, to get to know real customers and find time to listen to them?

And learning to listen means spending time doing it and finding ways that work and then acting on the results. The important point is that you have to develop strategies for listening and take active steps to make it work.

Making a commitment

■ ■ ■

The most crucial point, though, is to link the process and the skills of listening with a culture that says that listening is a good thing to do, something to be encouraged. You and your colleagues have to make a real commitment that you are going to listen to customers even if you have to make changes in order to do so. It's worse than useless for senior people to tell other people they have to listen and then for them to carry on telling, with no role modelling from their own behaviour.

Incidentally, if you still have any doubts about how important this is, just recall the last time someone failed to listen to you when you were a customer. Think about the impression it made on you and how you felt about it afterwards.

As with any change in attitudes or behaviour it will need leading. A listening culture and the development of listening skill must be role modelled from the top, a case of 'come on in the water is fine'.

The following is our way of presenting a listening cycle.

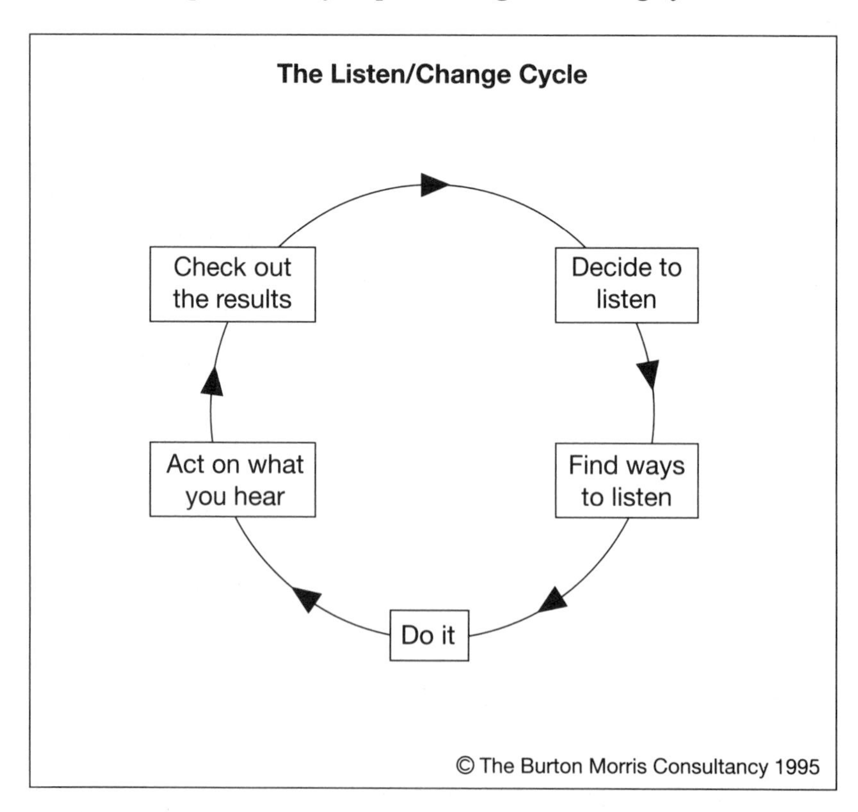

And as a brief warning note, this is what frequently happens if you don't go through all the stages in this cycle.

THE BELLY OF AN ARCHITECT

Recently a senior manager at a housing trust interviewed architects for the job of redesigning one of London's large estates. The estate is less than pleasing on the eye – not to say a downright eyesore.

The architect confidently started the interview by saying that the estate should be levelled to the ground because there was no community spirit. To which the interviewer asked 'Have you actually ever spoken to anyone on the estate?'

'No', came the reply, 'but just look around. How can there possibly be a community in a place like this.'

The architect had made a serious error. The senior manager ***knew*** there was a community spirit because she had ***spoken*** to tenants and spent hours in consultation meetings with them. They banded together in adversity and the environment produced an even stronger bond than in many 'nice' suburban areas. Sure, people didn't like the architecture – after all the last bunch of architects hadn't taken the time to listen to people properly either – but there was definitely a community.

People in fact had developed a community almost floor-by-floor in the blocks and there was also a strong community based on the estate's three churches.

Sadly for the architect he went belly up at the interview and wasn't appointed.

Making the cultural transition

■ ■ ■

Very few people are lucky enough to work in a company that is actively committed to getting to know customers. In most cases the chances are you will have to make some changes in order to create a more listening culture.

The process of assuming you know what customers want is often very deeply ingrained and has built up with years of custom and practice. It may have worked fine in the 1960s when there was much less choice and competition, but times have changed. It is probably for this reason that the 1980s saw the development of a range of management approaches, like Total Quality Management, which stressed the need to radically rethink the organization and focus all efforts on getting to know the customer and then deliver what they wanted.

Some organizations still find it really difficult to believe that listening to customers will improve service. This is especially true of those in monopoly positions, and to an extent the 'traditional' public sector, which have felt disinclined to get to know customers. The council had a contract for life to empty your dustbin, so there was no consumer power. Compulsory competitive tendering and privatization have hit that notion on the head, very hard indeed.

If it were just the monopolies, you might understand it – but it isn't. The madness grips even commercial companies, in tight competitive markets. How many times have you gone into a private company only to find they have no understanding of what you require and no intention of taking a blind bit of notice of what you are looking for.

So, the chances are you have some work to do. The trick is to take the steps gradually and help your people feel more positive about listening to customers. Winning an early success always breeds other successes.

Taking these steps involves many aspects.

Letting go of your fear of surprises

Sometimes listening to customers will simply confirm what you already knew – that you are offering an effective service, for instance, or that you are completely in tune with their wishes. However, you will need to welcome nasty surprises as well.

As the saying goes:

'If you aren't happy, tell us. If you are ... tell your friends.'

So if you don't get surprises when you listen to customers then either you:

- aren't listening hard enough
- are still doing too much talking
- aren't asking the right questions
- aren't asking the right people
- don't really want to be surprised.

If people are allowed to express their feelings and opinions in their own way and on their own territory they will often come up with surprising ideas and insights.

This means asking open questions, allowing people to be critical without fear of retaliation and being prepared for some painful home truths. It means realizing that not everyone holds the same views and priorities as yourself. Don't just wait for evidence to appear, confirming your views. Like Sherlock Holmes, search out clues and hints which may lead you to new ways of seeing things.

THE HOSPICE

A hospice prided itself on its caring attitude towards the people in its care. Middle managers decided to ask people what they did and didn't like about the care they received. There were surprises.

The most striking thing that came through was that patients didn't like the way nurses and other staff insisted on calling them by their first name. For many older people this represented a lack of respect and they would much rather be known by the more formal Mr or Mrs. For the nurses, first names meant being informal and friendly but this isn't how the patients saw it.

It is now policy to ask patients what they would like to be called and then to go along with their wishes.

Again, think about this in terms of a relationship between you and your customers. A relationship has gone stale if you are never surprised – and when this happens the chances are the other partner will start to look elsewhere.

Accept that there will be something worth hearing

If you don't believe you have something to learn by listening to customers then all we can suggest is that you close this book and go and do something else. You've seen it said before, but with no apologies for saying it again ... if you don't want to know the answers, don't ask the questions.

Be aware of the barriers

It is important to understand that customers have traditionally found it difficult to speak to organizations and consequently often don't bother.

So the listening manager is always looking for new ways to listen and therefore to understand.

We look in more detail at the barriers a little later.

Prepare for change

Understand that a commitment to listening to customers and understanding them, and taking action based on this understanding will mean some kind of change taking place.

The basic act of deciding to listen to the views of those, who in the past may not have been listened to, is about a change in attitude.

For staff, listening to customers may mean learning new skills or unlearning bad habits – like arrogance or indifference towards customers. If you embrace the listening approach then counselling skills and interpersonal skills training could become second nature to your organization. Listening to customers also means being available when they want to talk and this often means evenings and weekends. Listening, or as it is known in some quarters – consultation – therefore, could mean changing work practices.

At an organizational level new structures may need to be put in place – new committees, panels or even local groups for instance.

The sum effect of listening can be to change the way people and the organizations they work in behave. A listening culture welcomes comments and is not defensive.

Listening can help open up organizations and make them less bureaucratic.

Breaking down the barriers

■ ■ ■

One of the first steps you can take in order to get to know customers is to break down some of the barriers that keep them and their views away from you.

Many managers see management as a way of insulating themselves from customers. Some give a sigh of relief as they leave the hurly burly of the front line and move upstairs to the relative peace of the office. Some then do everything to keep themselves away from customers. However, this is a mistake. Today's manager must consistently look to get in touch with customers and understand what puts them off from making contact with their organization.

The following are just some of the barriers it is important to be aware of:

- ***Fear.*** Yes, simple fear. Customers often feel fearful of coming forward and expressing a view about the service. This is often the case when the person feels the organization has power over them – for instance many local authority tenants don't complain because they feel they might be persecuted as a result.
- ***Inertia.*** Customers have lives beyond the service you provide. They have families, go to clubs, go to work. So in order to get feedback you need to get beyond this and actively encourage them to come to you with their comments. We look later on at how customer panels can help you do this.
- ***Cynicism.*** If customers have made comments on the service or products before and nothing was done as a result why should you expect them to waste their time and give you feedback again?

- ***Geography.*** If your customers are not close to you geographically they will find it hard to give you feedback unless you help them. Companies do things like sending out questionnaires and phoning customers and taking out the organization to the people in order to overcome problems of geography.
- ***Culture and language.*** Listening to customers means listening to all sections of your customers. Some customers don't voice opinions because they don't speak your language or come from a different culture. One way through this barrier is to provide a translation service.
- Those ***nasty attitudes***. The following is a true story. It might give you an idea about why customers are sometimes shy about coming forward.

'WHERE'S WALLY!'

One large organization had a customer care department whose brief was to help customers who had a problem – or at least it was in theory. Over the years a culture had come into place that was completely disdainful of customers. They were wallies and the staff were always right. They kept a Wally Book in which were written down all the alleged stupid complaints. Nobody answered the phone unless they had to, and managers came in for a Wally Up-date.

Small wonder, that they didn't get many repeat calls ... or enough repeat business.

Do the following check

- **Do you have any jokey or derogatory terms for:**
  - **customers in general**
  - **certain groups of customers**
  - **awkward or difficult customers?**
- **Do you or your team talk disrespectfully about some customers to other customers?**
- **If a customer complains are they treated:**

- as a threat
- as a nuisance
- as someone providing an opportunity to learn?

- **How easy is it for a customer to get their views to you and your team?**
- **Do you go out of your way to listen to customers?**

Obviously, the answers any customer-friendly organization will give are quite straightforward.

Good organizations:

- do not invent a language of customer disdain
- do not speak disdainfully about customers to other customers
- make it easy for customers to make comments
- treat complaints as a learning opportunity
- go out of their way to listen to customers.

Setting up a formal feedback system

The get-out-and-talk-to-customers approach can take you so far, but it is only a start.

In order to really get to know your customers you need to set up an on-going formal system that can bring in customer feedback regularly.

This kind of formal system also makes a statement about your organization and department – that you want to listen. And if you are seen to want to listen then customers will talk.

Plug in

All organizations receive feedback about their services all the time. This feedback comes from customers and staff in the shape of comments, suggestions and complaints. Some organizations choose to ignore this feedback. Others have decided to deal with it more systematically as part of a feedback system.

Although this process of dealing with feedback is often placed under the banner of a ***complaints procedure*** this is only part of the story. Complaints procedures *are* important, but the real answer is to welcome and encourage all types of feedback and to welcome it from staff as well as customers. This broader feedback model gives an important role to staff – both front-line and managers. Staff become the eyes and ears of the organization channelling customers' comments and complaints and making suggestions of their own for improvements in services.

Nobody's perfect; there's always room for improvement, and that's what you want customers to pinpoint for you. Complaints are just free market research, really.

Why set up a feedback system?

■ ■ ■

You may have to convince your team and your bosses that setting up a feedback system is a good idea. The following arguments should help to persuade them:

- In many ways the feedback that comes in from comments and complaints is the most obvious dialogue going on between your organization and customers. Because this kind of, often informal, feedback happens all the time, it is the most obvious place to start any improvement process
- Setting up a feedback system can be a low-cost option for starting a climate of listening. At its most basic, such a system needs to be simple, publicized amongst staff and customers. It has to have some method in place of collecting and analyzing the data that comes in
- The Citizen's Charter emphazises the importance of one of the key parts of a feedback system – having an effective complaints system
- Setting up a feedback system can be a vehicle for bigger

and better things. Setting up an effective procedure is a clear signal to customers and staff that you intend to be more open, intend to do things differently and that you welcome their comments about your service. Taken further, a feedback system can help cut down barriers between service provider and customers, change organizational culture and give rise to a variety of innovative posts and activities. It is also the first step in opening a life-long communication channel with customers

- The valuable information gathered from staff and customers about services can be used to feed into service design
- Involving staff in the feedback system is a way of improving service quality – they become the custodians of the service. Indeed staff are well-placed to carry out this role because they are often closer to customers' views than management. They can pinpoint what is wrong in a way that management often cannot
- By calling comments and complaints *feedback* this helps get away from the sometimes negative image of simply having a complaints system.

What does an effective feedback system look like?

■ ■ ■

There are a whole range of elements you can establish in your feedback system.

In the following three sets of examples you will see different approaches to the feedback system. Some work and some don't.

What does come shining through is that effective feedback systems:

- are open
- actively facilitate the involvement of customers

- are based on listening
- are backed up with training
- are regularly updated.

Read through the three examples and then ask yourself the question 'what did and didn't work in each?'

COMMENTS PLEASE

One particular large retail company decided it wanted to welcome feedback from customers who came into their shops. So, they established a variety of yellow perspex boxes prominently displayed. On each of the boxes were the words: 'WE WANT YOUR COMMENTS'.

This was backed up with leaflets and some staff training. Staff were trained not to fear comments (at first they thought they would just get complaints) and to actively encourage people to make suggestions. Staff were also encouraged to contribute their own comments.

The company has made a vast number of improvements based on the system.

The following two true stories are how not to do it.

ON THE BUSES

A bus company in London started up a comments scheme. On each bus there is a tiny poster which says: '*If you have a complaint or comments about the service please write to …*'

Then there's an address – no name, just the address – and the bus company does not allow people to dial in their complaints and suggestions. Instead they expect people to find a pen in their bag and write down the address, probably while standing up, being thrown about in the rush hour traffic!

The chances must be that virtually no one has used the scheme. As someone standing at a bus stop was heard to say. 'Why don't they print the phone number on the back of the bus ticket if they really want comments? Why not make it easy rather than hard?'

The scheme is half-hearted and actually downright insulting and the company is likely to find out nothing of value from it about customers.

IT'S IN THE BOX

'My local gym has recently been taken over by an up-market company. It happens to now be a very good gym with excellent facilities – although it is pricy. The old gym had been losing members by the dozen because it was cliquey, unfriendly and if you made a suggestion or complaint you got shouted at or ignored – one man memorably alleged that he made a complaint, got no satisfaction, went into the shower only to be confronted by an irate manager who threw him naked into the street!

The new company decided to be more open and so started up a suggestions scheme. Good idea, but pathetic execution. The scheme was given no publicity, there was no clue as to what happened to the comments and the one suggestions box was just bigger than a cigarette packet and placed on the manager's desk.

I made a helpful suggestion to the manager. I suggested he got a bigger suggestions box.'

Learning by example

In the first example above, you see evidence of a good feedback system. For a start, the system is accessible. The yellow perspex boxes are obvious and displayed effectively. Customers know where they can make their comments. It also seems to work because it is clear from the system that the company is really interested in listening to customers. Indeed the company works on this by working on the publicity end of things, and making absolutely clear how to make contact. What's more, this is backed up with proper staff training, and by the actual culture within the organization.

There are no obvious disadvantages of the system, although if one wanted to be picky about it one could say that many people don't like writing down comments. In some ways having a system which married up a written suggestion scheme and a face-to-face scheme, where people could turn up, or indeed dial in their comments, would give a whole range of different approaches.

You have to remember that many people feel frightened or unsure about their writing skills, so any system needs to include a range of different options.

The second example is clearly a token gesture. On the one hand it is good that the bus company is at least acknowledging that people may have complaints. It's also good that the bus company realizes that it isn't just complaints that might come in. People might also have positive comments or suggestions. However, the fact that there is no name to contact, and that it is very difficult to get all the details down make this pretty much a waste of time.

The third scheme again has the smack of a token gesture about it. It's good that the company decided to welcome suggestions, but it is very unlikely they would get many.

An ideal feedback system

So the ideal feedback system will be broad and flexible. It will welcome all kinds of feedback – comments, suggestions and complaints. It will make it easy to make a suggestion in the way customers want to make it; by phone, in-person or in writing.

It will also include the following elements.

Consultation

It is all too common for organizations to decide to set up a system for listening to feedback and then hand the process over to an administration officer and tell them to go away and come up with some procedures.

Designing the ideal system should be a process of consultation in itself. This process should involve customers and managers and front-line staff.

Putting a user-friendly system in place

Following consultation, the next step is to put a system in place. It is important the system is easy to use for customers and staff. People will be put off using the system if they don't know where to start, or where the process will finish.

So the elements could include:

- suggestions boxes
- hot lines – where people can dial in and make a suggestion
- front-desk staffing – many organizations have arranged for middle and senior managers to sit on the front desk for a set time every month, so customers know they will get a hearing from a more senior person and senior people appreciate what is happening on the front line
- talking to a proportion of customers face-to-face each week about the service.

Training

The ideal system would realize the importance of training. Welcoming feedback, either through a complaints system or through a broader approach, means staff taking on a range of new interpersonal skills. For instance, they may have to use counselling skills or have to deal with conflict and will probably need training to develop or rediscover these skills.

A key component of training in this ideal world would be sessions to get inside what it feels like to complain or comment to a large organization as a customer. Such an exercise would focus staff on the barriers people face and which stop them coming forward.

The all-round advantage of such training is that it can help change organizational culture. Open and undefensive staff, prepared and given permission to talk to customers and empowered and trained to deal with their comments and complaints add up to an organization with listening in its marrow and not just in its procedures.

Information and publicity

Information and publicity are the lifeblood of any effective feedback system. Customers need to know how to make a comment or complaint, who to speak to, what they can complain and comment about, how they will be dealt with and what they can do if they still aren't satisfied.

The need to establish a broad information strategy to get people to come forward is also important. You may want to use adverts, local radio, newsletters, billboards or, even printing the number to ring on milk bottle tops.

The following is how one organization took its feedback system to the people.

THE LONDON BOROUGH OF LEWISHAM

The London Borough of Lewisham decided not to wait for comments and complaints to come to them, but to actively go out and seek them. This has happened under the banner of their quality commission.

The quality commission will identify a particular service to review. It then advertises the review in the press and invites comments or complaints on the service in question. Some of the people who write back are invited onto discussion groups. As part of the commission, centralized elected member's surgeries are publicized on posters in up to 2,000 locations, including High Street billboards. The surgeries are made up of councillors, senior officers and officers responsible for the service in question. At these surgeries, held in different parts of the borough, people are encouraged to come along and make their views and complaints known. The complaints brought up are then tracked and resolved and the information gathered is fed into a process of review, where departments analyze their procedures.

The London Borough of Lewisham have used their feedback system to widen the dialogue between themselves and their customers.

So, feedback systems are a good way of starting a dialogue with customers. The problem with them is that they are relatively narrow. The customer panels you looked at in the last chapter are another way of carrying on this sort of dialogue.

The round up

■ ■ ■

This section has looked at why it is so important to put in place an effective feedback system. By feedback we don't just mean complaints. We also mean comments and suggestions. All these can contribute to your organization learning about what it does well and what it does not do so well.

And when you have learned, you can do something about it. So this section has looked at a practical and effective way of putting in place this feedback system that will actually work for you.

In many ways we can see feedback systems as the Royal Road to Customer Relationships. Without them it doesn't matter what other high-tech system you put in place. It's unlikely to work. What you need is a simple system that actually acts as a kind of bedrock to your relationship with customers. A simple system that can handle complaints and suggestions and allow people to know that the suggestions are worth making is actually worth its weight in gold.

And finally, an example about this.

THE HOTEL NELSON

The Hotel Nelson in Norwich is a small hotel that prides itself on its ability to retain customers. In every room is a questionnaire designed to help people give feedback on the service. Unlike many hotel questionnaires, though, it also includes a little explanatory leaflet saying how much the company would value people's complaints, and if people want to comment in person, giving a name. However, the leaflet also lists examples of suggestions that have been made, and the way they have been taken on board. So it is for instance that we know that cus-

▶

tomers requested bigger towels, and hair drying facilities, and fresh milk in the fridge in each room. All these were comments that came in through the feedback system and we as customers know that they have been acted upon. Because we are told that some have been implemented, it makes us feel it is actually worthwhile making comments ourselves.

An object lesson, no less.

4

Observing customer and competitor behaviour

Stepping into the customer's shoes

At the heart of learning to love your customers is a need to understand the customer experience you are offering. And why? Well, at the heart of any service industry is simply the experience – *what it felt like*.

People have distressingly shaky memories. Ask them what they remember about a service and it isn't the features of the service they talk about – the number of cashpoint machines on offer or the number of options on the restaurant menu.

What they insist on remembering is the experience – that nice member of staff who sorted out their complaint, for instance.

HOSPITALS AND RESEARCH

A number of new NHS Trusts have carried out research into customers' perceptions of the services. The Trusts expected comments about big things like the way operations were carried out.

Instead they received thousands of comments from consumers about simple service experiences. The fact that it was difficult to park or that the receptionist was unhelpful or they had to wait for a porter.

When you accept this then it's a business imperative to go out and look for yourself, to test the customer experience and the competition being offered.

The challenge is the ability to step into the customer's shoes – into their experience – and see what if feels like. It's only then that you can really start to decide:

- what other competitors are offering
- why customers choose them
- what you can learn
- what new standards you can set for yourself based on this.

And this in a nutshell is simple, informal and everyday benchmarking.

So, what people remember is the experience they had and it's the quality of this experience that will help guide their decision about whether to use your organization next time around. And this to an extent faces everyone with a quandary. It is easy to get hung up developing the features your service or product offers. Indeed it sometimes seems more glamorous to develop the whistles and bells. However what those inconsiderate customers insist on doing is concentrating on the simple things – on things like the way they are treated and the care you put into the service.

It's for this reason that organizations are increasingly investing time and money to gain an insight into what that customer experience really is. Obviously, this can be done at least in part by talking to and listening to customers.

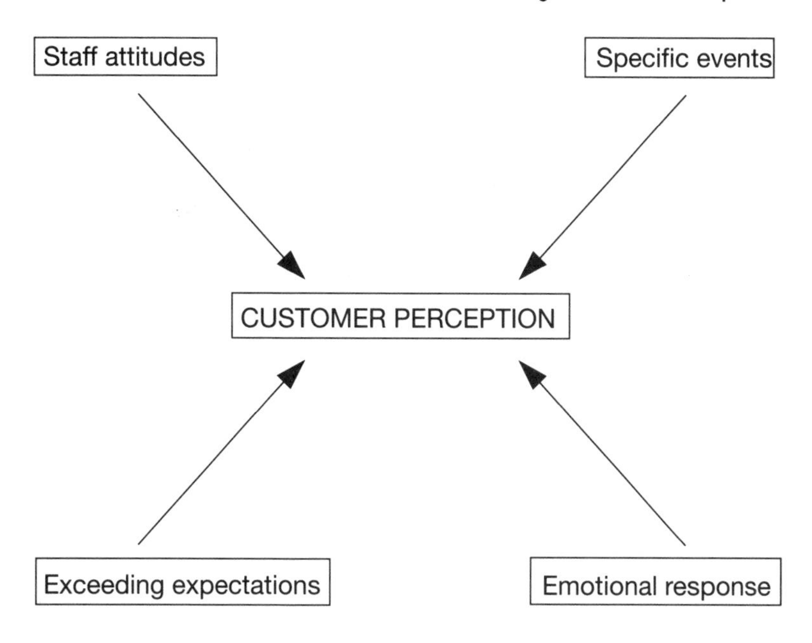

However, there is another area that is sometimes neglected – observing customer and competitor. One of the challenges for today's manager is to help their team to become experienced and dedicated customer watchers.

Think this through

It is easy for a kind of continental drift to take place between manager and customer. Sometimes under pressure of deadlines the customer can seem distant or even a nuisance. How close would you say you were with the customer experience of the service your team offers?

The key to getting back in touch is a spot of customer watching. Just think about how much you learn from watching, and naturally reading the signs.

Is everything all right with the meal?

Imagine you run a restaurant, and nobody has complained. Yet, out of the corner of your eye you spot a customer frowning, and pushing the food round the plate as if it was puzzling them. What do you read into this?

Do you say, 'Well, nobody said anything, so it must be fine', or do you go over and ask whether everything is all right with the meal?

Anyone with any sense goes over – and everybody would feel they ought to, even if they bottled out in case they encouraged a complaint. But, as you saw in an earlier chapter, complaints are free market research. Putting things right now could very well save you a customer, avoid an ugly scene if they get angry later, get them back in future, and get them to tell their friends how well they were treated.

Do some customer watching

■ ■ ■

Customer watching is often either written off or overlooked. However, this kind of evidence acts as free market research and can help develop your understanding of what customers are really looking for. It pays to always be observing your customers and the customers you might have who are at present with your competitors.

Of course, armed with the information you can get in this way, you can then develop your own service to reflect customer needs more accurately.

So the challenge is to develop your team into perfectly legitimate industrial spies.

In other words, your team needs to share your commitment to constantly find out what customers want, and part of this is the ability to keep their eyes open, to watch, and to come back with information as a result.

And where they need to do this watching is at home and, importantly, on enemy teritory. Going out and observing your competitors is an important way of benchmarking your service against them. It's one of the ways you can pick up tips and tricks that you can come back and apply yourself.

Why do it?

There are a number of perfectly good reasons why it is important to spend time observing customers in your competitor's environment.

It's simple

For a start, it's simple. The ability just to start calling in on competitors, and observing what they are doing, is something you can utilize immediately. However, you will need to work hard on getting your attitude right and being clear about what you are looking for when you visit competitors. With a little bit of training though, and some clear thought, it's not a difficult process, and it's something which you and your team can get involved in at once.

One of the keys to learning about your customers is having a diverse and varied approach. Successful organizations look for opportunities to learn the whole time, and this kind of informal benchmarking exercise is a useful and speedy way of starting you on the road to understanding your customers more fully.

It's cheap

Another advantage of this approach is that it's cheap. You don't need to pay a market research company. You simply build up new skills within your staff at low-cost.

The only real costs you are likely to incur are if you decide to give your people time off to go and visit competitors.

It can be part of a more general learning programme

There is a thrust in today's world towards learning organizations – in other words organizations that actively seek to plug into their people's learning and improve the company as a result.

Another reason why this kind of research is important is that you can use it as part of a more structured programme to help your team understand where your organization has come from, and how it has developed, and where it needs to aim for in the future. As such you can use it to help staff put your company into context and be more reflexive practitioners.

A structured approach to benchmarking by your team is one way of gradually developing awareness – about the business, about the customers and about the future.

In this book we look time and time again at the need to create an on-going relationship with customers. One way of doing this is to develop an on-going programme for understanding more effectively.

As you follow the steps in this chapter you will be able to develop an integrated, informal benchmarking programme within your team. Of course, the word team is important and another reason why it is such a good exercise is that it can help involve **you and your** team in a shared endeavour. If they feel that everyone is pulling in the same direction, and everyone is making more of an effort to find out more about customers, then the whole exercise can be much more effective.

It can be carried with you

Another reason why this is a useful exercise is that you can help develop a skill that will stand your team in very good stead. What modern managers want is an empowered team each of whom possess a **portable** critical faculty. Customer watching is portable.

It's stressed in many modern textbooks that you don't want people to switch off their brains when they come in to work. Implicit in this is that you want people to switch **on** a critical faculty. If you can encourage people in the simple and straightforward way to start observing competitors and the behaviour of customers, then you are helping to develop this portable critical faculty.

It helps you to see the world afresh

One useful concept is that of defamiliarization.

What this means is that common everyday objects, events and behaviour, become so deeply ingrained that we no longer notice them. In organizational terms this may mean that we perpetrate the same poor service against customers time after time without even realizing it. An exercise in putting yourself into the customer's shoes is one way of allowing us to see the world anew – or defamiliarizing it

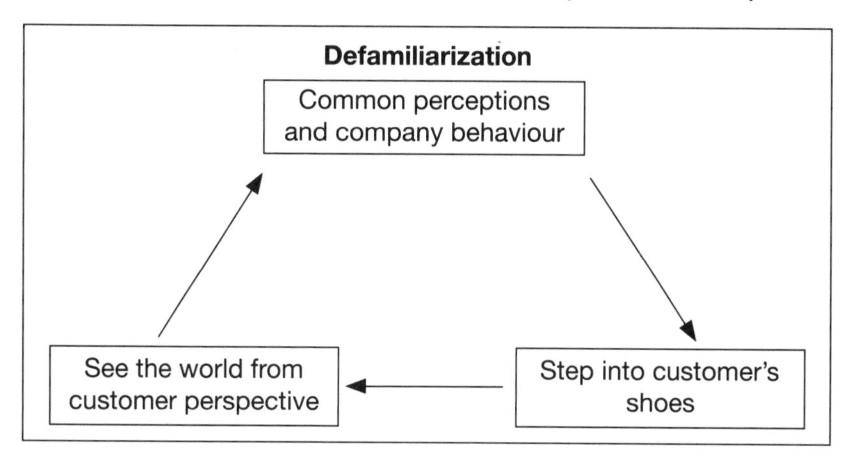

When we have done this we can start getting a true feel of what it's like to be a customer, and why they do or do not make the choice to come to our particular organization. So one of the reasons for getting your staff out and into your competitors' businesses and observing customers' behaviour is to help them see the world afresh, from the customers' viewpoint. It's only when you do this that you can really start focusing intently on what they want, rather than what you want.

What is it?

There are a number of important techniques for observing customers' and competitors' behaviour, and we will look at three in detail in this section. The key to each is the desire to experience things from the customer perspective.

The three areas we look at are:

- ***Informal benchmarking.*** This involves doing some research into your organization, identifying your competitors, and then going out and seeing what customers are getting from these organizations.
- The use of ***mystery customers***. Many organizations use mystery customers to come in and test their own service in order to get a real feel of what the service feels like to customers.

- ***Customer secondments and placements.*** Another technique for getting a feel for customer perspective is to actually allow your staff time to go and work for your customers so they can get a real feel for the way that you yourself behave.

The first thing we will look at in this chapter is informal benchmarking.

Informal benchmarking

Running a structured programme

The way we will approach informal benchmarking in this section is to present an entire programme for it. Of course, it isn't absolutely essential that you follow the whole programme, although it is desirable. If you want to you could start this exercise from Step 4 onwards.

However, we think it is important to put this kind of exercise into context. All too often when people visit competitors they aren't exactly clear what they are looking for, and don't take all the factors into consideration. If this happens, the information you get back is likely to be rather unhelpful.

You need to be clear about:

- what you are looking for
- what criteria you are using
- what you intend to do with the information.

So if you can find the time, the best way is to take a slightly more leisurely instructional approach and build it into your systems. There are three broad areas in this approach, although we will break these down into more steps later on.

The broad areas are:

1 ***Getting a clear idea about what your market is,*** and where you are now as an organization. It's only when your team can successfully position themselves, and see where the organi-

zation fits in, that it's really possible to go out and discover what competitors are doing, and what customers want.

2 ***Going out and doing some research.*** There's no substitute for actually getting out of your office or business or organization, and getting into other competitor organizations to find out just what they are doing, and to start observing the way customers behave there. This means that although you need to do some planning, and it's important to get the conceptual basis, the real meat of this exercise has got to be in the actual visits themselves. So make sure that if you take this route you leave plenty of time to actually go in and experience what customers are experiencing elsewhere.

3 ***Using the information.*** It's no good visiting your competitors if you simply come back with either a long wish list, or a list of things they are doing wrong. The most important thing about this information is to come up with tips for improving your own service and to set some standards as a result.

We look later on at how one organization did this.

So, the stages in a structured approach to informal benchmarking are:

- explaining the process and winning your people over
- putting your business in context
- investigating your local area
- getting your mental attitude right
- identifying your competition
- visiting the competition and making observations
- using the information.

Using a seven-step approach

■ ■ ■

This seven-stage approach should ensure that you get the full picture of what your competitors are offering, and start to get genuine insights into what customers expect and indeed are being offered elsewhere.

Step 1 – Winning your people over

It could come as a bit of a shock if you suddenly announce that you are going to visit the competition and carry out a benchmarking exercise. For a start the word benchmarking has a touch of jargon about it, and could easily scare the pants off your people. Also people may suspect your motives or simply see the idea as a silly new fad or a waste of time. You need to take your people along because you can't really do the exercise without them.

The key really is to explain why it is you believe this to be important, and what exactly you are looking to get out of the exercise. What you need to do is persuade your people that it actually is part of the job to learn from competitors, and that it's important to let one's own preconceptions go. All too often a kind of blinkered mentality creeps into organizations, and it can be hard for employees to realize that other people may do things better, and at the very least we need to look at things from the customer perspective.

So, call your people together and explain to them why you want to do this informal market research. You will probably need to explain that they have a key role to play, and you will need to explain about any support you think they will need. If you are intending to use the information you get to help you improve your service, you will also need to spell out clearly the kind of process you are going to go through, in terms of making recommendations for improvement. Some organizations have completed the following kind of exercise as part of an ideas and suggestion scheme.

FORTE POST HOUSE

When Forte Post House carried out this exercise they produced a leaders' guide for all the managers running it. The guide included a set of slides explaining the advantages of this process, and explained the main outcomes the company were looking for. Managers were urged to hold question and answer sessions and to encourage people that this idea was both valuable and a way of finding out some useful information.

It took a number of months to go through this customer watching induction across the whole company.

Step 2 – Put your business in context

It's all too easy to rush through this exercise, and go straight to the business of visiting competitors to see what they do. Try not to be impatient, the preparation will be worth it.

It's important that you and your team have a clear idea of where your business is, and how it got to where it is today. It's only with this background information that you can actually start slotting in the experiences of your business. You may in fact find that there has been a change that has affected the whole nature of the business. The aim here is to give a very brief history lesson, to get a feel of how the business is developing.

The following checklist may help you do this.

Some ideas about how to research the history of your organization

1. **Talk to long-serving and ex-employees.**
2. **Dig out records.**
3. **Look back over local press cuttings.**
4. **Dig out the figures for sales and profits.**

The important thing here is to get a broad map of where your organization slots in.

You may well find that there have been either some seismic changes over the last few years, which themselves may have a bearing on the way your competitors act, and what they offer, and what customers expect. Changes can affect:

- who the competition are

- what customers expect.

The following are just some of the examples that have happened in the public and private sectors, each of which would have had a bearing on customer expectations and competitor offerings. If you don't manage to get a handle on these, it's difficult to put any information you find out into context.

CHANGING TIMES AND EXPECTATIONS

In local authorities there has been a move to compulsory competitive tendering. This means that many services are now contracted out and that councils are organized very differently to the way they were a few years ago. This in turn may well have had an effect on the expectations of customers of council services.

Any benchmarking activity would need to take these changes into account.

This kind of change also has an impact on who you are likely to identify as your competitors. Just ten years ago it would have been impossible to see councils in these terms. But these days a whole range of leisure and health and other facilities may well be directly competing with the kind of services that councils offer.

Competition in supermarkets has become cut-throat. There has been a move to out-of-town shopping and this has had a damaging effect on many supermarkets in city centres. The public have become increasingly food aware and are often looking to try more premium products. These factors alone are likely to have an impact on what the competition is offering, and what customers may well expect. Different patterns of shopping, and different expectations all form part of the background of any benchmarking exercise. Again, it is also useful to identify your direct and indirect competitors.

Step 3 – Investigating your local area

In the same way that major changes in the history of your organization are likely to affect the way customers perceive your service, the same is true of changes in your local area.

Any changes in your local demographics are likely to affect the type of customer you have access to, and the kind of services your competitors are likely to be offering. If they are ahead of the game and have a broader and clearer picture of the local environment, they may well already be offering services that are encouraging your own customers to defect to them.

So it's important for any modern manager to build up a clear picture of what's happening locally. This is true even if you work for a large chain or brand. Local knowledge is an important way of plugging into the aspirations of your customers, and, of course, the offerings of your competitors. There are a number of things you can look out for in your local area. These include:

- the general location. It's important to be aware of any geographic or demographic factors affecting your local area. You need to ask yourself whether anything has changed or is likely to change, that will affect the expectations and kind of customers you have available to you
- have there been any changes in the patterns of class or home ownership? Has the community you cater for changed in any way? These are all-important, and it's vital to draw a map that will help you be clear about what's happening in your local environment. The following checklist should help.

A checklist to investigating the locality

1. **Collect demographic information from the local authority planning offices.**
2. **Watch the local press for planning applications. Get out and about in the local community.**
3. **Visit local events. Drive a different route to work to investigate the social mix of the area.**
4. **Ask yourself questions like: who is likely to use us and why?**
5. **Start a scrapbook of relevant articles from the local press. These could show things like firms that are coming into the area; firms that are closing; any competitor news.**

All these things will help you get a clearer picture of what is happening locally. In many ways this is the canvas on which your competitors are painting their own business.

And of course it's against this background that you will be able to start the next step, which is to identify your direct and indirect competitors.

Step 4 – Getting to grips with the competition

The main necessity is to be clear about who your competition is. When you have got a picture of this you can start visiting your competitors, and working out the experience they offer to customers.

It's important to think not just about your direct competitors, but also your indirect ones. In today's increasingly competitive market place, competitors can spring up quickly, and you need to be always on the lookout for possible threats.

This stage, in which you identify your competitors and get to grips with the competition, has three distinct steps:

1 Identifying the enemy.

2 Understanding why customers choose to go to them.

3 Observing what customers do when they get there.

Identifying your competitors

The important thing is not just to concentrate on looking at the direct competition and ignoring the indirect threats.

For instance, consider the leisure industry. These days, if you run a cinema, your competition isn't just other cinemas. It's also anything that offers people the chance to spend their disposable income on leisure. So the indirect competition could even include things like local garden centres.

So when you come to draw up your list of who your local competitors are, and who you are going to research, it's important not to just look in the obvious places. Try to be creative, and try to get a feel for where customers actually go.

The next checklist will show you how to draw up your list of competitors.

Identifying competitors

1 Draw up a list of the obvious direct competition. You will probably be pretty clear about these already, but it's worth talking to your team about who they see as direct competition. When you have a list of names, write down some of the indirect competition that you can think of. Again, it's a good idea to involve your staff in these matters.

2 Ask your customers where they go to, and what other people they choose in the same kind of work as you. You may run this list alongside the list you have drawn up with your staff earlier. The chances are you will come up with some surprises here and indeed this is one of the ways you may start to identify your indirect competitors.

3 Have a staff gathering to run through competitors. They may well use or visit similar organizations to yours through choice. Again, here you can draw up a list of direct and indirect competition.

4 Use a drive-time approach. It's important to be realistic when identifying the competition and in being clear about how far people will travel to use your service. Obviously, the distances people will travel will depend very much on things like location and the kind of business you are in. But it's worth drawing up a drive-time boundary around your organization beyond which you think people will not usually travel to use your services. For hotels the drive time is seen to be about 20 minutes. So, when they are drawing up a list of competitors, a hotel will draw a line around any business outside that 20 minute time frame.

Why do customers go to them?

It's worth preparing in your mind a few ideas about why you think your customers visit your competitors. You may well be able to draw up a preliminary list of some of the attractions that are on offer, and some of the added value elements of the service. It's important not to close your mind, because when you get to it you may find your initial ideas confounded, but at this stage it's well worth drawing up a broad list of why you think people actually go to the competition. You may even be able to carry out a bit of quick market research among your current customers. Why not ring three or four customers you know and ask for their views on why they do, or do not, choose the competition, and what the competition really is.

Step 5 – Get your mental attitude right

This is crucial, and in some ways is where the real benchmarking begins.

Where people go wrong in benchmarking exercises is to go in with a whole list of preconceptions. There are number of very damaging things you will need to avoid, which are:

- becoming complacent. It's easy to think that you are simply the best organization and that it isn't worthwhile checking out the competition. It's important to realize you mustn't rely on what has happened in the past, or any obvious advantages you have – for instance location

- writing off the competition. This is the main danger. Never underestimate the competition. They are always capable of surprising you.

'I tell my people when they do this they mustn't act as a kind of silent assassin. It's very easy where you're in a particular world to become hypercritical about what everyone else does. That won't do you any good when it comes to benchmarking. I tell people what they really want to do is to go in and find out what the competition are doing right. Sometimes people have come back and said to me that one of our competitors was really full, in fact much fuller than we were, and then give me a long list of the things they were doing wrong. I just say they must be doing something right.'

Marketing Director, retail chain

This is a useful notion, and is one that you should take with you when you go out on a benchmarking exercise. You need to go in with a positive attitude.

The aim when you have identified your top competitors is to find out what they are doing right, what customers see in them and why customers are continually going back to them rather than coming to you.

So the key is to ignore any minor annoyances and ignore the things that you think are important, but obviously aren't important to customers. The key when you go in is to be able to pick up on the experience that is being offered to customers, and being able to articulate that when you get back. It's important to realize that customers are often not as sophisticated as the professionals who run businesses. They sometimes aren't that worried about some of the nitty gritty issues, but are much more impressed by the broad brush strokes. This probably explains why people are prepared to queue for hours to get into restaurants like Planet Hollywood just to say they've been there.

So when you go in to benchmark the important thing is to try to tune in to what customers are thinking and actually observe what the competition is doing that is giving them that all important advantage.

Step 6 – Go visit

So, you've done your preparation, you've worked out who your competition are, both direct and indirect, and you have got your mental attitude right – you are going in looking for the positive.

The next step is to actually go visit. Remember, what you are aiming for is to get a feel for the customer experience that your competitors are offering – not just the features.

Pick a representative team

Rather than just going yourself, get a mix of different people together so you get a whole range of different perceptions.

This means that your team could/should/might include:

- you
- someone with young children
- a single young person

- a middle aged person
- someone from one of the ethnic minorities.

If you choose a spread of different people it will allow you to get a range of different experiences and perceptions of what your competitors are offering. What you want is to choose staff who represent the same kind of customers you want to attract, or those that use your existing service. This will mean that the feedback you get will actually give you a real customer insight as well as a staff insight.

But what do they do when they get there?

Clearly you need people who are going to come back with some sensible feedback. One mistake people often make with a benchmarking exercise is to send people off with either a very long covert questionnaire, or far too much to try to find out. Remember, you don't have to do everything at once and it's much better to come back with two or three important ideas or innovations that you can actually use.

So it's important to discuss beforehand and be clear about the outcomes you want, and these are just some of the questions you might arm your people with:

- what do the competitors do well?
- why do customers come here?
- how good are the staff?
- what will make customers come back?
- what experience is the competitor offering?
- what is their unique selling point?

The key is you want your research team to spend time with your competitor and actually observe what customers do and how the competitors offer an effective service.

It's important to stress again that you are not looking for your staff to go in as assassins. What you want is for them to come back with a list, or ideas in their head, about the experience being offered and what customers are noticing.

Of course, when your team come back with their feedback it's important to do something with it.

Step 7 – Using the information

You might want to call a meeting when you have collected the information, to pull together the kind of findings you are coming up with. When you have done this you will have come up with a list of recommendations, for instance:

- things you can do today
- simple service standards you can adopt
- things that will take more time and cost more money. The important thing is not to let the information go to waste, but show that the exercise was worthwhile. If you send some people off to do some benchmarking, and you ignore their findings, they won't take it very seriously.

A word about benchmarking

The word benchmarking can cause confusion, but what it means basically is the ability to set standards based on your competitors' performance. So when you get back information the key thing is to use it; set yourself some service standards, or come up with some tips or innovations you can actually do in practice. A benchmark is just that. It's a mark. It's just what it sounds like. It's a marker against which you can measure yourself.

So your competitor analysis should allow you to come up with a whole range of ideas and standards that you should set yourself in your own organization.

The following is how one company actually uses the information it gets back from this kind of exercise.

'We did this exercise and we did it on a regular basis. Every month at least one of my staff would go out and visit one of the competitors, and then come back with a report to us.

What we did with this information was to set ourselves what we called "hot tips". In other words, we put together pretty simple and straightforward things we could do as a team that would plug in to our perceptions of what customers wanted, based on our research. We would come up with new hot tips every month, and see how they worked, and what effect they had on our business. It was important to give the whole process a focus and that's what hot tips allowed us to do.

We weren't just faced with a load of information we didn't know what to do with. We were able to use it to improve the service. Calling it hot tips also acted as a tremendous motivator for people. Eventually all of them were competing to come up with the best hot tip, and help us improve our service.

The important by-product is that I now have a team of people who are always on the lookout to learn what customers really want. I've also managed to get beyond some of that professional jealousy people feel towards our competitors.

We are no longer just looking at them and trying to pick holes in them. We look at them and make our minds up that we are going to be just as good, and better than them, and that we are going to put ourselves in customers' shoes and walk around in them.'

Mystery shoppers

There are other ways of getting to the customer experience as well as the benchmarking exercise above. However many of the same principles still apply.

You need to be committed to getting a balanced and objective view of the service – although this time it is your own service you are measuring.

You may have seen advertisments on TV that centre on the Ansell's Mystery Customer. A publican smartens up the approach when it's suspected that one of the customers is a 'spy' from the brewery. Mystery shoppers are another way of stepping into the experience of your customers. Mystery customers are essentially people you plant to help test the experience people get from you and your team.

What can you use them for?

You can use mystery shoppers to test things like:

- the level of product knowledge your staff have
- how your staff deal with awkward customers
- how your staff deal with customers with special needs – for instance people whose language is not English or people with disabilities
- how promptly your staff deal with customers
- how your staff deal with unusual requests
- a particular service area that has generated complaints.

How does it work?

The mystery shopper will be briefed to test a certain aspect of the service. If they are operating by phone they will have a list of questions to ask. If they are visiting in person they will have a mental list of things to test.

To staff, of course, they appear like any other customer. This is the beauty of the idea because they can genuinely test the customer experience in this way. When they have visited and gone through their routine they will then draw up a report on the experience.

Here is an example. The phone rings. It's answered within 15 seconds. An impatient caller is calling Royal Mail to arrange for his post to be redirected. A delivery officer gives the appropriate advice. The customer rings off.

Nothing unusual in that, surely? Well, no, until you realize that this 'customer' already knows the answers to the questions asked, because the information is right in front of him. This is not some elaborate hoax: the caller is a mystery shopper, secretly testing customer services.

Public and private companies nationwide are finding that the mystery shopping technique can complement surveys to gauge customer opinion about their services. Of course, if you really want to find out what customers think you have to ask them, but mystery shoppers can provide a new dimension and a way of testing the customer experience.

One of the reasons mystery shoppers are so powerful is that it is a sad fact of life that customers are more likely to complain than praise, and more likely to forget improvements than defects. What organizations need is a more objective evaluation of its services. Questionnaires can work well, but the problem with them is people find it difficult to know what benchmark they should be comparing the service against. Mystery shopping can't solve this kind of problem, but it can give a kind of controlled test of customer perceptions.

An example of using mystery shopping is the Royal Mail, which employs an external agency of mystery shoppers to test its customer services. Royal Mail use the mystery shopper method in conjunction with the questionnaires they give out to customers. For instance, the Post Office gets about 6,000 completed questionnaires in each Division every month. If questionnaires reveal poor scores in one particular area, for instance callers and delivery officers, they can then send in mystery shoppers to actually find out what the problems are. The North West Division of the Royal Mail uses mystery shoppers in all its 200-odd delivery offices but uses an internal team rather than an external company. With this approach the shoppers call and ask a range of basic questions about services. They judge the speed the phone is answered, the responsiveness, the courtesy, and the knowledge of the person who answers and the information that is given out. For the Royal Mail this has been an important way of testing customer perceptions and gives them a way of rapidly testing out any problems that seem to be emerging.

TEST VALLEY BOROUGH COUNCIL

Test Valley Borough Council is one of twenty-six local authorities which use an agency to assess staff responses to enquiries from the public. Callers ring ten times a month, tape the conversations, award marks for performance, and then submit a monthly report along with the cassette. The council also uses its own staff as mystery shoppers. John Spence, Assistant Director of Housing, explains:

'As well as external assessment one person in each department is detailed to monitor colleagues' promptness in answering internal calls for a fortnight, six times a year. They write down every call they make, and whether or not it is answered within three rings. It works really well.'

PIZZA EXPRESS

Pizza Express, the Italian food chain, also tests its own operations. This time, though, it doesn't use mystery shoppers, it invites long-term customers to tick off its check list rather than paying researchers. The mystery eaters report on every aspect of the business, from the cleanliness of the pavements outside to whether they were bid farewell on leaving. John Metcalfe, the Group Operations Director, says:

'They do it for the love of pizza. They seem to have a more real concern about our business than people who are paid to do it, because they understand what we are about, and the level of service they expect from our restaurants.'

So mystery shoppers can be a useful way of service testing.

Working for customers

The final approach for stepping into the customer experience is to actually go to work for your customers, and look at the experience you are offering from that perspective.

This can be a very powerful experience because it gets you out of your own environment and helps you see things from the customers' point of view.

What often happens is that people see how their companies' actions unintentionally cause problems for customers.

There are in fact a whole range of methods here, which include:

- secondments
- customer visits
- job swaps.

The idea behind this is that if you go and work for a customer you will get much more insight into the customers' problems and insights into any hitches or glitches that are occurring with your service.

Secondments

Do you have any opportunity to arrange a secondment of one of your staff to be one of your customers? This is often an option in the public sector but is increasingly spreading to the private sector as companies build up a more partnership approach.

Visiting your customers, or asking them to visit you, is an extremely good way of finding out more about them. You may want to take it a stage further and offer to place one of your staff in your customer's business as a secondment. The advantage of this is that you learn much more over a period of time about the business. Also, it allows you to get a more genuine picture of what their business is really like. In essence, you get the whole picture rather than just a snapshot. This approach is often taken in government departments. When the Department of the Environment decided it ought to do something to provide funding to help house people sleeping on the streets, it invited a number of representatives from housing associations to work for a year at the DoE to establish a sensible policy, and oversee its operation.

Secondments show a commitment to your customer, and a genuine desire to find out what their requirements really are. More than that, it gives you an opportunity to gain an invaluable insight into the daily operations of your customer.

By offering an exchange, you can also ask your customer to send one of their staff to come and work with you for a period of time as well. When this happens, you may find yourself moving towards a strategic alliance.

Customer visits

The simplest way to keep in touch with your customers is to visit them or to invite them to visit you. It allows you to see the customer in their own environment and find out more about them, both in a structured way and also in an informal way.

The aim of any customer visit is to build on your knowledge of their business and the way it operates, and also to build on the relationships you have established with key members of their staff.

Rank Xerox, for example, set their salespeople the task of meeting ten customers per day. Across their organization, this means that there are thousands of customer interactions every single day. When this information is collated, it gives Rank Xerox a wealth of knowledge about what their customer needs are, how their customers perceive the service that Rank Xerox provides, and what their customer needs are likely to be in the future. This gives them a distinct competitive advantage.

But it's not only about gaining a competitive advantage. Inviting customers to visit **you** can be instrumental in changing your customers' perception of your business and how it operates. The following example was given to us by a public sector manager who is responsible for the procurement of new housing projects.

> *'One of the large building companies we worked with had a reputation for being uncooperative about making changes once a building contract was on site. I couldn't understand this as we were obviously prepared to pay for any changes we made. I was invited to visit their offices and, because I had a meeting there on the same day, reluctantly agreed. I had a busy day ahead and the idea of touring a company's premises did not fill me with a great deal of excitement.*
>
> *However, it was an extremely enlightening process. The company are different to some other construction companies in that they build houses in almost a conveyor belt fashion. They have pared the process down from initial design through to the working drawings through to the site operation so efficiently that any minor change requested at a late stage completely throws their system off track. More than that, they are competitive because they have this*

pared down system, and any change eats into what are already slender profit margins.

From thinking of them initially as uncooperative, I left with not only an understanding of their system, but also an immense amount of admiration for the way they operated in such a cost efficient way. It made me recall why Fairview had won the contract in the first place: they were considerably cheaper than their rivals, whilst offering a very similar product.'

So customer visits are a crucial way of:

- gathering information
- understanding the experience your team offer from the customer's point of view
- showing a commitment to your customers
- being visible and available.

And to do it? Well, you need to show a commitment to listening and give your team space to get out there and watch and listen. You also need to come up with a sensible mechanism for using all the information you gather. People need to feel it is worth making observations based on a customer visit. And the main thing you should do? Well, make a change as a result of the visit. Improve things and keep improving things. And when you have improved things tell everyone that you have made an improvement and tell them what.

SPENDING A DAY IN THE LIFE OF YOUR CUSTOMERS

Tony Cram, author of *The Power of Relationship Marketing*, quotes an example of one company who took this approach and learned a great deal. The example is of the Weyerhaeuser Saw Mill at Cottage Grove, Oregon, USA.

'The general manager of the saw mill arranged for a cross-section of employees, from himself to a fork lift operator, to go for a week at a time as employees of customers. They were there to look, listen and learn. They returned full of practical ways to make their customers' lives easier . They began colour coding

timber ends, loading lumber in the way that was easiest to unload at the other end. Telephone sales personnel and field staff better understood customer problems, solved and even anticipated them. Buying from Weyerhaeuser was easier and sales rose. This is a particularly good example because it shows just what happens when you do step into someone else's shoes in this way.'

Job swaps

The idea of job swaps has been around for a long time but mainly only in terms of internal job swapping. Of course this is useful because it can help you to see things from the perspective of your internal customers.

However you may also be able to job swap with one of your external customers.

And finally ... strategic alliances

Some organizations are so bound up with their customer that they have made a strategic alliance. They have decided to commit to each other in a symbiotic relationship, with joint benefits for both parties.

The Body Shop, for example, holds joint strategy meetings with its suppliers, particularly its transporters, to work out how to improve the business. In this case, the transportation companies are not merely sub-contractors to the Body Shop: they are partners in a joint venture.

This partnership approach may well be one to watch for the future. It certainly allows customer and provider to really understand each other and make commitments to each other.

There are barriers to this like:

- overcoming fear that the partner will gain a competitive advantage
- different company cultures can clash.

However the modern company and customer relationship may look like this.

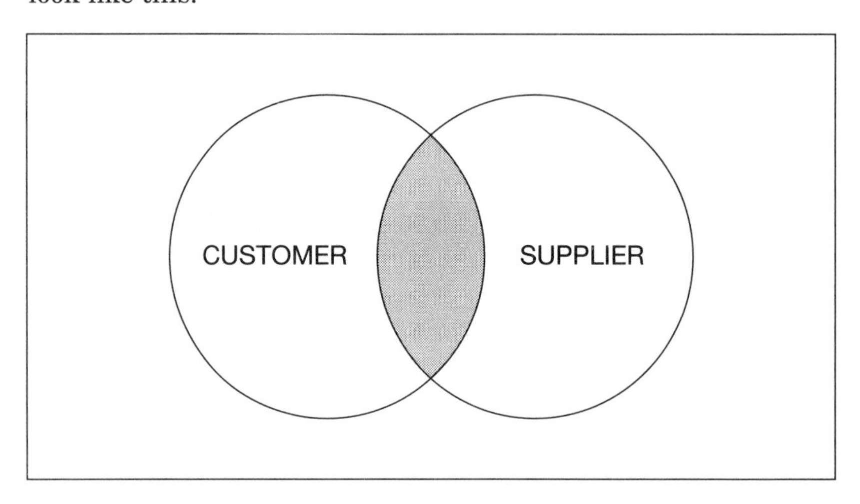

To round up

In this chapter you have looked at the vital business of understanding the customer experience – of stepping into the customer's shoes. There are many ways of doing this – ranging from informal benchmarking to strategic alliances. From this kind of exercise comes:

- understanding
- closeness
- continued contact.

What all the approaches have in common is the understanding that these days companies really need to work at understanding the customer experience. They can no longer simply assume they know what customers think. And everyone in the company needs to be involved. It isn't just the job of the strategic planners and marketing department.

Acting as perfectly legal spies is a serious business and one everyone should adopt. And when you've done the spying set some standards based on your findings.

5

Keeping in touch with your customers

Can you survive the death of marketing?

So far we have looked at a number of ideas for getting to know customers better. We promised you, though, some cutting edge ideas at the beginning of this book. And the idea that might actually change the way you really view your customers is that simple, traditional marketing is no longer enough.

Traditional marketing relies heavily on identifying customers, finding out what they probably want or probably want to hear and then targeting messages at them. Many companies have looked at their relationships with customers this way. The way this idea goes is that if we can find out who our customers are, and the kind of product they are likely to buy then we can sell it to them using a leaflet or a letter or the like.

As Regis McKenna in his article 'Real Time Marketing' in the July/August 1995 issue of the *Harvard Business Review* points out:

> Marketing executives are not used to thinking about how to build and manage dialogue with their customers. Marketing has long been a broadcast discipline, rooted in practices developed for selling mass produced goods to broad homogenous markets.

And for marketing executives, read organizations and the managers who work for them. All too often people have thought in terms of sending out publicity of spreading the good news, rather than a set of more radical propositions like:

- Why don't we try to really get close to customers?
- Why don't we work interactively with them?
- Why don't we really involve them in an on-going way in the service?
- Why don't we see customers as individuals?

And it's new technology as well as new thinking that are helping to open the doors to this new reality. Put simply:

Old marketing is as dead as a doornail.

112

Start simple

This chapter is the first of three looking at how to really develop lasting relations with customers. In the last of these chapters we look at some high-tech and leading-edge ideas. However, at heart, many of the ideas are simple and have been around as long as people have traded.

So a simple first step is to start by taking the trouble to learn your customers' names. Obviously this is tricky if you have thousands of customers. But if you can put a name to a customer then they become a person and it's people that we can develop a relationship with that lasts.

'THANK YOU ... I KNOW YOU'

Many firms have started the practice of using customers' names. You may recognize this example from your own experience. It comes from an off-duty researcher who called in to the MFI store in Haverfordwest, in West Wales.

She was impressed anyway, by the way the staff offered to help if needed, without pushing. Having made a choice and tendered her credit card, the sales assistant said '*Thank you, Mrs X*' and used her name.

'It made such a difference. A Canadian lady who had been served just before me, said they knew her name too, and what a wonderful place this was and how impressed she was with the quality of the organization.'

And all because of someone reading names from a card.

A simple test

Before you start on this chapter try the following simple test. Write down the names of ten of your customers. Now write down the names of the last five customers you were in contact with.

How did you do? If you remembered all the names you are doing very well, but if you only remembered a few, then you are not. All too often people don't take the time and trouble to remember their customers' names. It's a simple point, but it certainly has an effect.

If you aren't taking the trouble to remember your customers' names, then the chances are that deep down you haven't made the psychological shift to valuing them. So make a note and get your memory working. It's extremely powerful if the next time that customer rings up you can remember what they are called, or the next time they come into the office you have still got their name on the tip of your tongue.

The following are a couple of true examples: one very good example, and one very bad one.

MARN HANWELL

Marn is a car dealing and garage company. It deals with all kinds of different makes of car, and at the Marn Hanwell branch has a long established servicing and garage operation. The two managers have been with the company for a number of years, and always make a point of learning customer names. When a customer visits the garage the managers remember the customer and always greet them using their name. This can even

▶

happen after four or five months gap between the last transaction.

This personal service and nice touch really gives the feeling that the garage cares about customers. The managers may well not have thought this through as a policy, but naturally or instinctively it actually works very effectively.

THE LOCAL SOLICITORS

I contacted a local firm of solicitors to draw up my will. I had already used them to do the conveyancing on my previous house. I got on pretty well with the solicitor, and she seemed competent enough. However, mysteriously, when details of my proposed will came back the solicitor had got my name wrong. I didn't take much notice of this, after all, these things happen. I corrected the will and sent it back, and it came back about three weeks later.

The name had been corrected, but to a different name, not mine. This was despite the fact that I had written clearly on the first draft my correct name. About a week later another letter arrived informing me that this particular solicitor practice was merging with another and they were looking forward to keeping my business, and maybe offering me a wider range of services. However the letter was addressed to a third name, again the wrong one.

I phoned up to say that if they couldn't be bothered to get my name right, then I certainly wouldn't be using them again!

These are two local examples, and you can probably think of plenty of similar examples yourself. But if you fail the name test, then I'm afraid it's a case of 'do not pass go'. You are never likely to build up any kind of long-term relationship with a customer if you can't even remember their name.

In many ways this kind of approach can be characterized as 'wham, bam, thankyou Maam'.

Building a good relationship with customers

■ ■ ■

There is an increasing realization of the need to understand customers, to keep them loyal, and to orientate your business around their wishes. Throughout this book we have looked at some of the ways of getting closer to customers. In this chapter we will look in more detail at how to start the process of building an on-going, strong and successful business relationship with the people you provide goods or services for. In the next chapter you will look at some more sophisticated methods to help broaden the customer relationship.

The important thing to realize is that it is an increasing fact of modern organizational life that customers need to be kept and wooed. Indeed, Ind Cope Retail, one of the UK largest pub chains, include 'customer woo' as one of the main features required by successful managers. Broken down, 'customer woo' means possessing the ability to understand what makes customers tick, and keep in contact with them.

If we just open our eyes, examples of this new organizational perspective are all around us. Each can teach us something. The following are just three examples that show how the business of developing relationships with customers has moved very much to the forefront. As you read though them ask yourself how well you score on the customer relationship front?

The following message was spray painted on the back of a small company's van:

> T J WILLIAMS WOULD LIKE TO THANK PAST, PRESENT AND FUTURE CUSTOMERS FOR USING OUR SERVICE.

This was followed by the signature of Mr T J Williams.

T J Williams are a very small company. The chances are it is their only van, but what an important message to give out. It says to customers that T J Williams respects them and values them. It also goes beyond the bland mission statements, like 'Simply The Best' that one sees sprayed on so many local businesses' vans. What this says to us is that this company is intent on seeing customers as individuals and in developing an on-going relationship with them.

But it isn't just the minnows that have caught on. Unsurprisingly, big companies have also realized just how important the business of on-going relationships is.

Take Ford, for instance. Anyone who watches television, or listens to commercial radio will have heard the adverts of Ford over the last year. The key line is: 'EVERYTHING WE DO IS DRIVEN BY YOU'.

This is important. Ford didn't choose to say: 'EVERYTHING WE DO IS MADE BY US' or: 'EVERYTHING WE DO IS MADE BY HIGHLY SOPHISTICATED ROBOTS' as they probably could have done.

Instead the message is that the whole business is oriented towards what the customer wants. The business revolves around fulfilling customer expectations, and, more importantly, plugging in to their aspirations. Despite the rather nasty sound tracks to the adverts, the message is very clear. Ford have put the customer at the centre of the equation and understand that fulfilling customer expectations is at the heart of any successful business relationship.

The last example to start this section off is about the massive Heinz company. It's a remarkable story, and one we can learn a lot from. In particular it says a lot about the way the world is developing, although it has stoked up some controversy. It shows how one major company has moved resources into understanding customers rather than simply advertising **to** them.

In 1994, Heinz decided to stop spending money on traditional television advertising. This was a shock to some of the advertising companies, and also a shock to the industry as a whole. However, Heinz' logic was impeccable. They argued that television adverts simply cost too much and weren't specific enough. Indeed, with seven major categories of products within the group, including beans, soups and ketchups, placing adverts for each was a prohibitively expensive task.

But it wasn't just the expense that Heinz were thinking about. They felt that by simply concentrating on advertising they were losing contact with their customers as individuals. They may well have created a mass market, but they didn't really know what their individual customers were after, and they felt they had lost contact with them.

Heinz' response was to go for a more direct marketing approach, or as they call it, 'to concentrate on below-the-line activities'. What Heinz did was to concentrate on building up a magazine which they called *Heinz At Home*. This is now delivered free to four million homes on the Heinz customer database. It includes recipes using Heinz products, articles on new products, and a 'Kidz At Home' section.

The idea behind the magazine was it allowed Heinz to get in contact more directly with customers, and in the process start making them feel part of the Heinz team. The lynchpin of the whole exercise has been the desire to get people to respond and write to Heinz. Every page has something to encourage this. On one page there may be a special offer for kitchen mugs. On another page there may well be a recipe competition offering a prize: for instance a trip to Scandinavia. On another page maybe money-off coupons. Each coupon sent back in has a bar code which allows Heinz to identify the household that actually sends it in. And of course there is the ubiquitous letters page, opening up two-way communication.

This is ground-breaking stuff, and reflected a real change in the industry. It also showed that Heinz had begun to believe that the really important way of learning to love customers was to stay in contact with them, to keep in touch. The whole programme is interesting, because it encourages people to buy Heinz products, but it also stimulates massive responses. This can be seen as a genuine interaction between company and customer. In fact, the first two editions of *Heinz At Home* stimulated 1.5 million responses to offers and promotions from consumers.

Heinz took a gamble, the results of which can't yet be told, but it is important that Heinz felt that they needed to create an ongoing dialogue and an interactivity with customers. These next two chapters are about helping you, in whatever kind of organization you work, to go along this route. One of the key factors in Heinz' decision was they wanted to own their own customers, and keep in touch with them, to develop a relationship and stop the scatter-gun approach of TV advertising. There are arguments that by withdrawing from TV the Heinz brand may suffer in the long run. The jury is still out on this one, but the point is that big organizations are still striving to seem like small organizations to their customers. So whatever kind of organization you work for, the key is just to keep in touch.

Something to do

Having read the set examples, how much effort do you think:

- you
- your team
- your organization

put into developing a relationship with customers?

Why make the effort?

When your in-tray is overflowing and your telephone won't stop ringing, keeping in touch with your customers may seem like a luxury you can afford to ignore.

Organizations who can keep their customers coming back for more have the edge in today's highly-competitive market. Here is a quick reminder of some of the reasons why, covered in Chapter 1:

- when there is little difference in the price a good customer relationship may be the only competitive edge you have available
- it's expensive and time consuming to keep finding new business to replace lapsed customers. You are running to stand still
- rapid customer turnover creates bad will. Rumours travel fast and possible future customers will hear about the complaints and go elsewhere.

Today's consumer has never had it so good. Their options are infinite. An international array of companies and products to choose from and great value for money because there is so much choice. For example, look at the number of varieties of mobile phone that are available in the UK today at a price to suit every pocket – ten years ago they didn't exist.

Companies need to take every initiative to out-perform their rivals. The loyal customer is your trump card. They are one of the most important commodities a company can have, defining the real value of your market share. The more long-term customers you have, the larger and more secure your hold on the market.

The truly loyal customer is less likely to take their business to one of your competitors. Trust and confidence are difficult factors to quantify, but they are well worth cultivating. When a customer takes their business elsewhere, you may not lose just one sale – you may lose their business for life.

A loyal customer keeps buying your products or services and helps you to hold a steady share of the market. If you can predict a proportion of your annual business, it's easier to forecast and plan developments for the future.

Contact with the customer gives you the chance to learn. Honest and open feedback from your customer can help you develop the products the customer wants. This can increase your sales and help your organization focus on the customer's real needs. Keeping in touch with your customer should make your job easier.

Relationship marketing – the cure for all ills?

■ ■ ■

Management is laden down with terminology. New fads arrive; some managers surf on them, but jump to different fads as soon as they arrive. We shouldn't be distressed by the level of language changes in management, it just reflects the fact that management is a vibrant changing activity. But at the moment, one of the important phrases in management is relationship marketing.

This book isn't specifically about relationship marketing although it does inform some of the thinking here. Over the last few years relationship marketing has been cited as the answer to almost all our problems. It's been seen as the way of keeping customers for life and building up relationships with them.

So, how do you keep your customers coming back for more? How do you build a relationship with your customer? Every organization wants the answer to this question.

Tony Cram, in his book *The Power of Relationship Marketing** defines it as:

> **The consistent application of up-to-date knowledge of individual customers to product and service design which is communicated interactively, in order to develop a continuous and long-term relationship, which is mutually beneficial.**

A health warning

However it is important to know that with all panaceas, relationship marketing included, there are dangers. One of the problems is that the terminology simply gets out of control. Another is that the claims for different ways of looking at the world become so outlandishly high that anyone with any sense realizes that it just simply can't deliver. A recent article in *Management Today* explains just what happened to the language of relationship marketing:

> Already (relationship marketing) is commonly equated with loyalty schemes, direct marketing, database marketing or all three. Sending out a piece of junk mail has become 'opening a dialogue'. Sending out six pieces of junk mail over a year has become 'deepening the relationship', while offering bribes to keep consumers from defecting is, of course, 'rewarding them for loyalty'.
>
> (June '95)

This doesn't mean that building a relationship with your customer is a bad thing. It is just a matter of how you do it. If you

*Pitman Publishing, 1994.

listen to your customer's opinion and act upon it, this probably will be appreciated. Drowning them in so much junk mail that they cannot open the front door is unlikely to make you popular.

Remember you are not the only company sending them information. In 1989, the average UK household received 35 pieces of direct mail; today they receive 80. The average American gets up to 950 pieces per year. That's why it's called junk mail!

It helps to keep reminding yourself that you too are a customer. Think about how you would hope to be treated, how you would react to this approach?

Not all your customers will want a relationship with your company. People value their privacy. Don't force yourself on your customers, you will only alienate them. They will take their business elsewhere.

Why keeping in touch with your customers works

Previous chapters looked at how learning to understand your customer can improve the service you offer. You will learn even more about the customers' interests and needs by nurturing this relationship. This way you don't simply rely on a snapshot impression from a single business deal. You understand their needs as they develop.

In this chapter we will look at what turns a first time buyer into a loyal customer. We also look at how companies have gone about keeping in touch with their customers, examples which might help you keep your customers for life.

VAUXHALL

If you buy a new Vauxhall car in 1995 you will not receive the standard booklets, facts and figures that you used to receive. Vauxhall decided that they want to get people communicating with them, and get their customers to feel more a part of the Vauxhall way of doing things. So when you buy your new Vauxhall you get a leather-look binder. Every month you then have the opportunity to send off for chapters to go into the binder, featuring useful facts and figures, and useful information. These include things like:

- first-aid tips
- good restaurants near motorways
- the best beaches in England
- where to stay in southern England

and so on.

The idea is that this becomes a handy reference source. For motorists it is essential, and it all comes in glove compartment size. It's nicely presented and professional, and written in a friendly way. However, it performs more than one function, because as well as giving good information to customers, it also increases customer loyalty. At the end of two years of collecting the different chapters the time will be ripe for Vauxhall to send a letter to customers asking them whether they would be interested in a new car. What's more, it actually encourages vast numbers of people to start writing to Vauxhall.

This is one of the big challenges for big companies. How do you get people to make contact with you when you may well be perceived as impervious and impersonal. The Vauxhall scheme is a way of creating customer loyalty, and creating customer contact. It also creates essentially what is a gift of high quality and a gift that will be appreciated by customers.

So the key to start the relationship developing is:

- to get customers making contact with you (it's much more effective then sending out junk mail)
- help them to feel part of the club
- offer them things they want.

The personal touch

But keeping in touch is about more than just sending out interesting fact sheets. It is about giving the personal touch and caring enough to do something a little special.

We are all customers of one type or another. Although we know we are not the only ones in the world, we all like the idea of receiving personal service. We like to feel unique.

Big organizations strive to be like small organizations in the way they keep in touch with their customers. This helps to give the feeling of personal service – the traditional approach of the old fashioned shopkeeper, a trusted friend. The more you learn about your customer, the more you can provide exactly the service they want. The problem is how to go about it?

So, although in the next couple of chapters we are going to look at some innovative, new and high-tech ways of keeping in touch with customers, it's important to keep the simple truths close to hand.

What customers really want is to feel special and to feel that you care about them. What's more, customers will know if you aren't being sincere, and any amount of successful marketing or leaflets, or anything else, won't cover up for some very simple aspects of customer service. You need to make customers feel special and feel cared about. To use the relationship metaphor, a relationship doesn't add up to much if you don't show you care.

Successful organizations always try to find little ways of showing they value customers, and all their staff are committed to this idea.

The real live customer test

Think of five things you or your company have done recently to make a customer feel special. Then write down five things which have made you feel like a special customer.

If your two lists match maybe you can claim that you really understand your customer. The chances are, however, that you selected two very different sets of examples.

All too often the specialist manager chooses incentives, mail shots or extra gizmos, whereas the customer opts for polite personal service, convenience and reputation. The former are all very well, but customers won't be swayed by them unless they get the quality of service they expect as well.

Tony Cram* suggests that there are six essential factors which a customer wants from any relationship:

- **3 Cs** – convenience, cordiality and consistency (these get the consumer to pick up the phone in first place)
- **3 Rs** – relevance, relationship and reputation (essential to close the sale).

The Automobile Association and the RAC have recognized the power of the 3Cs in their advertising campaigns. The AA's 'He's a very nice man' advert focused on how AA mechanics offered service with a smile. No task was too difficult or inconvenient. The RAC opted for the knight in shining armour (or bike leathers in this instance). On call day or night, rain or shine, to dash to the customer's rescue.

Other companies have chosen to highlight the 3Rs. Prudential Assurance, for example, ran a campaign featuring all sorts of different people thinking about what they wanted to be. The implication was that the Prudential had a policy which could help you buy your house, become top striker for Liverpool FC or travel the world. They could offer the customer a relevant relationship that the customer could trust.

The advertisers and marketing executives believe these factors matter to the customer; so should the manager. Bear these factors in mind whenever you communicate with your customers.

Something to do

How do you match up against the 3Cs and the 3Rs? Give yourself a mark out of five for each.

- 3 Cs – convenience, cordiality and consistency
- 3 Rs – relevance, relationship and reputation.

**The Power of Relationship Marketing*, Pitman Publishing, 1994.

The good old days

Also remember that things change. Just because you consulted your customers once doesn't mean their views won't alter.

Don't get complacent and continue to trade on past glories. Customers aren't obliged to want the service that you offer them. They are at total liberty to change their minds, something you will only know about if you keep in touch.

PEOPLE POWER

When Clive Sinclair invented the Sinclair C5, he hoped to revolutionize the world of personal transport. No reason to suspect he wouldn't get it right. Sinclair's laptop computer, designed and priced for the home user when computers were a rarity in the office, made him a millionaire.

The single seater car answered many prayers: electrically driven, it was good for the environment; capable of driving at 35 mph, good enough for most short trips; small enough to park with ease in crowded town centres; and simple to drive.

So why did the Sinclair C5 become one of the greatest marketing flops of all time? The customer wanted to be safe. The C5 was small and sat low on the ground. It left the driver feeling vulnerable and exposed. People didn't buy the C5 because they didn't feel safe in it.

Most car manufacturers during the 1980s spent millions of pounds developing ever better safety features for their latest car models. It was what most customers said they wanted. It is still true in the 1990s. Customers want safe cars – air bags and ABS are now standard on many inexpensive family cars. The C5 by contrast vanished without trace. Two years after its launch C5s were being offered, by the thousand, to Bonhams as novelty lots for their Christmas auction.

Keeping in touch with customers, consulting them, asking them about what they are looking for from your service isn't something you just do as a one-off. It's not an activity you carry out, write up, present to the Board or to your manager, and then put in the filing cabinet and forget. It's really a process and something you should be doing all the time, and it should be ingrained into your people. It isn't something that you fit in when you are not too busy to do your real work. So, one of the keys to success in this area is to make consultation, listening and keeping in touch a way of life, accepted by your people as an enjoyable part of their job, and your job, and everyone else's job.

Some important do's and don'ts

It's a tricky balancing act, fulfilling your existing orders and still finding the time to concentrate on building the relationship with your customers.

So, as you embark on this chapter and the work and ideas it throws up, it's important to get into your mind a set of Do's and Don'ts. They are not prescriptive and you may be doing different things that actually bring about the same end result. The important thing to remember is that you do need to work at making your company as open and accessible as possible. We look at this later in the chapter. It's important also to think through the whole style of your relationship carefully.

Too aggressive, too false, too brief, too lavish and you will end up looking stupid or arrrogant or both. So get a picture of a customer in your mind and match the style. Don't start with the style and match the customer.

The following is an example of when a company didn't do this, with the disastrous consequences that can result.

> *'When travelling on an airline I saw the senior steward kneeling down beside a passenger. At first I thought he was offering first-aid, or something, but it turned out when I walked past that he was in fact questioning the passenger about the service. Question was in fact far too mild a word; it sounded as if he was interrogating the passenger. His face was about two inches from the passenger's face, and he was asking staccato, difficult questions about the service. When he had finished he moved three chairs up the line and did the same thing to that passenger. He then moved on three further chairs up the aisle and did the same thing again. Obviously he had been told he must consult people and listen to them. However, the steward had not thought through at all the*

style of relationship he was looking for with the customers. Instead this person was carrying out a mechanistic, almost policing role. He wasn't clear what the company wanted, and the company wasn't clear about what he was doing.'

Checklist

The following list should help you think through some of the issues.

Do:

1 Make it easy for the customer to tell you what they think, good and bad. People may complain but they very rarely tell you that you are doing a wonderful job unless you ask.

2 Set up systems to keep in touch with your customers which are fully integrated into your team's daily work programme. Try to build a relationship in a haphazard way, without specific systems in place that take care of themselves and your efforts will be in vain. We'll look at this issue in more detail throughout the rest of this chapter.

Don't:

1 Intrude, threaten, bribe, bully, cajole – no one needs to put up with it and your customers will leave you in their droves.

2 Expect people to be monogamous – variety is the spice of life.

Building on the first steps

■ ■ ■

In the rest of this chapter we are going to look at some simple first steps in building up a relationship with customers.

The idea of building a relationship can come as a bit of a shock, particularly in organizations that are used to having a more snapshot approach to customers, or indeed organizations that really have no conception of the kind of relationship they want with customers.

However, as you work through the rest of this chapter you should be able to begin picking out tips and ideas that you can start to use yourself. This chapter, though, looks at some of the basics, some of the simple things you can do, and these are all bound up with the basics of learning to communicate more effectively.

It looks at:

- working out some team tactics
- opening up dialogue
- writing to customers.

Team tactics – running a happy ship

There is a simple truth involved with creating a relationship with customers. Happy staff make happy customers. What's more, you need to work hard at helping your staff to feel part of a team that is fully committed to getting to know what customers want, and then operating on that knowledge.

This is how one manager in the Health Service described the effect of Total Quality Management (TQM) and how it helped him and his team make contact with customers again:

> *'The thing about TQM is that it puts people back in contact with customers. It got everyone to focus on customers, to talk to customers, and to find out what they wanted. An interesting by-product of this is that people came up to me to say that for the first time in about 15 years they were doing what they came in to the Health Service for – to get close to customers. TQM, for all its faults, rekindled in my staff the very reason they entered the Health Service in the first place. For that reason it was very useful.'*

You may not have introduced TQM, or indeed any quality initiative, but whatever you do the important thing is to rekindle that obsession with customers, and rekindle the desire to get back in contact with them again, and build up a longer-term relationship that will help you keep in touch with them.

However, if you don't manage a happy team, or if your team feel demotivated it's very unlikely that whatever you say, you will be able to develop a relationship with customers. If your team feel undervalued, or that you don't listen to them, the chances are they won't listen to customers, or have much interest in them. It's true that sometimes in circumstances of extreme adversity people still manage to keep up this on-going relationship with customers, but it's rare and it's not something you can rely on.

The following are just some of the things that are in favour of creating a team approach towards developing a customer relationship:

- so much of what we talk about in this book is about attitude – your attitude, customer attitudes, and the attitudes of your staff to each other. If the attitudes are right, the motivation is good. Then you can start building an organization that has customers at its centre
- happy staff will do things for customers, and when you do something for customers it's an expression of the esteem you hold them in. Returning to the initial title of this book, you might see the business of staff doing things for customers as an expression or a token of their esteem in this relationship.

The following is a good example of how happy and empowered staff are the cornerstone of learning to love customers. It also shows just how important a team approach is.

SABENA

A customer wrote to a business magazine recently describing the service he received on a SABENA flight to Belgium. Apparently he got on the flight, only to discover he had left a crucial agenda to the meeting he was heading off to in the SABENA terminal. He told one of the cabin crew. The cabin crew member made contact with their desk at the airport, and managed to find the agenda, and get it on to the next flight to Brussels. They then taxied it over to the person's meeting, and managed to have the agenda on the customer's desk 15 minutes before the meeting started. He wrote in to say how pleased he was with this.

This splendid example encapsulates what other writers have striven to put down in entire books. The organization was empowered to focus on customers. The staff cared enough about customers to actually do something special for them. And when you do something special for a customer, they remember it and tell their friends. What the SABENA team did was turn the words the company issued about believing in customers and wanting an on-going relationship with them into action.

If you can take a leaf out of the SABENA book the chances are that you will be putting in one of the cornerstones of any on-going relationship. If your staff are able to do something special for customers, then of course you will be able to develop and broaden the relationship between your staff and your customers.

The challenge is to put staff in contact with customers.

You as a manager are part of this process. You need to champion customers, and show your staff it is all right to do more than they would normally do, but it's not all right to be indifferent, rude, or uncaring towards your customers.

Above all you need to make sure you put staff in contact with customers and that you keep in contact with staff.

The Royal Walkabout

Meeting the people is not an activity reserved for The Queen. All managers should do it.

Take 15 minutes out to walk around your office and say 'hello' to your team and internal customers. Stop and chat with a couple of people each time. You don't need to chat to everyone you see but make sure you talk to different people each time.

You will be surprised how often people take the chance to say things to you in passing. This helps to nip problems in the bud. If someone says 'This customer is causing me a real headache...' you can either solve the problem on the spot or, if more appropriate, arrange to talk about it at the next team meeting.

You can also use this technique on the sales floor. Talk to a customer briefly (once your sales staff have closed the sale!) and ask them what they like about the product they bought. This keeps you in touch with the customer and lets your team see you behaving in the way you want them to. Lead by example.

Team tactics – attitudes towards the customer

We have already talked about how important it is to get the attitude right. Above all, it's important that staff need to see that getting feedback from customers is a crucial part of their job. It is indeed one of the main cornerstones of this relationship you are aiming to develop over time. More importantly, it is one of the few things that will sustain it.

Many more traditional marketing books concentrate simply on the business of customer information – finding out what customers want. And it's important to keep in touch, to listen, to learn, to consult. But that really is only part of the equation. Without happy and committed staff, all the listening will be to no avail. The following company obviously didn't see customer feedback in this crucial light.

'FLY ME – I'M DREADFUL'

A former hotel manager always requested a customer feedback form whenever he took a long-haul flight. The form, a pen and his old business card sat on his tray and remained there throughout the flight. This technique usually guaranteed superb service, probably because the stewards thought he would report any misdemeanours to the tour operators.

One day a friend mentioned a terrible experience he had with a particular airline. The manager was surprised, he had always rated that airline highly. So the next time he flew he decided not to ask for a feedback form. The service was dreadful. He felt as if he were a tiresome inconvenience to the steward.

Half way through the flight he asked for a customer feedback form – suddenly the steward could not do enough for him. Too late, the bad impression had already been made.

Ideally, customers will never come face to face with this situation. Managers should tackle the attitudes behind such behaviour before they get out of hand and alienate loyal customers.

Here are some steps a manager can take to ensure his or her team has the right attitude :

1. Ask your team for their views. What do they think their customers want? How do they listen to customers? How do they think they could provide a better service? Create a brainstorming culture where all ideas are worth mentioning. You never know when a really good one will emerge.
2. Take a team member along to your next customer visit so they can see how the customer operates.
3. Invite key customers (internal or external) to give a quick talk about their role and the part your team play in it.
4. Encourage staff to take pride in their work – everybody has an impact whether they clean the floors (creating a good environment for workers and customers) or design the product.
5. Check the staff handbook backs up the positive message that everyone plays a part in keeping the customer satisfied. Get the message across on the first day and hopefully it will become instinctive.

Team tactics – getting involved.

When keeping in touch with the customer, your team's involvement is crucial to success. Even if you don't run a sales team we all have customers – the people to whom we send work or report. Your team is the front line.

If the manager can encourage staff to treat customers like individuals, the customer will know they are getting the personal service they deserve and keep coming back for more.

All Sainsbury's staff now wear badges saying 'How may I help you?' Your team also need to be driven by the motive to give the customer what they want. Here are some ideas for how managers can involve their team in keeping in touch with the customer and help create a positive atmosphere for feedback:

- have a clear rally call – 'we want to give the best and fastest pizza delivery service in town'
- tell everyone when a customer says thank you – and congratulate the staff who made it happen at the next team meeting or in the staff magazine
- ask staff to watch out for competitors' developments and put press cuttings on the notice board
- nominate a customer champion within your group. Get your team to pass on ideas for improving customer relations to the champion. Also any feedback from personal contacts, friends or even something they overheard in the pub for consideration at team meetings
- offer your front-line staff training sessions in telephone skills or negotiation
- create an award scheme. You should reward staff for positive customer commitment
- empower staff to take ownership of customers. Stress they are their customers and you won't come charging in to take them away. When people have ownership they tend to get closer to customers.

Jan Carlsson, the Chief Executive of SAS Airlines, summed it up :

> *'If you are not directly serving customers you need to be serving someone who is.'*

Working through the virtuous triangle

Finally, in this chapter where we have concentrated on some simple ideas and the importance of staff in the whole process, it is important to put things into perspective.

In many ways looking at the staff angle is one prong of a virtuous circle.

You should look to tackle all three prongs to really get close and stay close to customers. One without the other may leave looming gaps that can undercut all your good work.

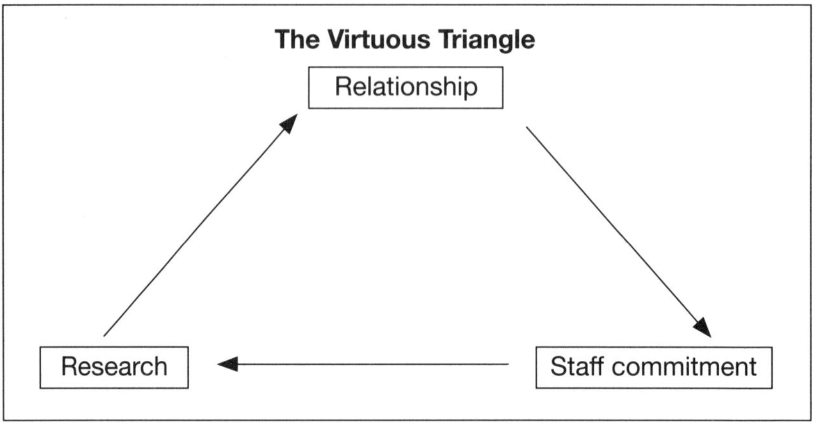

The Virtuous Triangle

Relationship → Staff commitment → Research → Relationship

To really be in touch with customers you need all three.

You need to research – which we looked at in earlier chapters – to help you understand customers. Some market research tends to get stuck at this stage.

You need the relationship – which we look at in detail in the next two chapters – to keep customers coming back.

You need to encourage staff to make the relationship happen. It is the staff who really deliver the service and it is the service itself that demonstrates most clearly your commitment to customers.

The round up

In this chapter you have looked in detail at why it is so important to build up an on-going relationship with customers.

You have seen that the basis of this relationship needn't be complicated or high-tech. It is built on respect and trust and a series of simple drills you can go through.

It is also crucially bound up with the staff you have in your team. If they believe in putting customers first then you have a chance. If they don't then it is going to be uphill all the way.

You need to work at developing staff who are committed to listening to customers and offering them a service that really shows you want them back.

6

Developing a dialogue with customers

Rising to the challenge

If you're like most managers the following questions will have exercised your mind.

How do we develop a real dialogue with customers?

How do we really get them to talk to us honestly?

How do we talk to customers in a way that really reflects the esteem we hold them in?

If you're like most managers you probably found the answers difficult to come by. In this chapter we will look at ways to help you to get answers.

Getting your customer to talk

Opening up the dialogue

The crucial lubricant of any relationship is dialogue. Without it, we have suspicion, distrust and mutual incomprehension.

Remember Fawlty Towers? Remember Basil Fawlty saying 'Yes?' to a guest in that inimitable and testy way? The same word, used with a smile and genuine display of interest, has a positive effect. Basil could never have been accused of that.

It's very important to somehow encourage customers to talk to you. This can sometimes be difficult because customers can't see the point in making contact, especially with a big company, because they think nothing will happen.

The key thing is to start breaking down the perception of you as an impersonal company or service provider, and for customers to see you as a series of individuals with whom they can talk, get on with, and continue to do business with.

So the heart of any relationship is the ability to open up your company, and give access to customers.

British Home Stores have stressed that they are a friendly place by using actual customers in their TV adverts. This stresses that everyone is part of a big happy BHS family.

How do you score

Answer the following questions to see how open your department and organization are to dialogue:

- How many letters and phone calls does your department receive from customers each month?
- How easy is it for customers to make contact with you?
- Can they dial direct?
- Do you answer every letter you receive from customers?
- Have you worked at making your letters friendly and human in tone?
- Is your office customer-friendly?
- Is it clearly signposted, is there access for people with mobility difficulties, and so on?
- Do you actively encourage people to make contact with you in the way that suits them, rather than the way that is convenient for you?

Score well on these and the chances are you already have a reasonable level of dialogue with customers.

Score badly and the chances are you appear like the Rumanian Secret Police to your customers. And your place of work is not somewhere they are likely to make contact with voluntarily.

How organizations have encouraged dialogue

Walk into a bank now and it's very different to the bank of just ten years ago. In the old bank all staff were deposited behind bullet-proof or glass screens, and customers had to queue up in order to talk to the staff. There was definitely a 'them and us' attitude at the bank.

Around ten years ago the banks decided to make themselves more open organizations. They wanted to open up the branches and visibly demonstrate a new approach to the banker/customer relationship.

Walk into a modern bank now and there will almost certainly be no screens except where cash is handled. There will almost certainly be more effective queuing mechanisms, and there will definitely be staff out and interacting with customers. The banks have realized that the heart of a banking service is interaction and relationship, and are actively trying to encourage this. They also encourage staff to learn selling skills so that when people come in they can offer a range of products. Coupled with this has been the move to open up the back office part of banks so that it can be viewed by customers.

All these changes have meant that the bank is no longer seen in quite so impersonal a light and has helped to create a more **open organization**.

The important thing is to allow people to talk to you and companies have invested much time and money into making themselves far more open.

The next guide is one we do not recommend you follow.

The ten-point devil's guide to talking to the customer

1 Never be available at evenings and weekends.
2 Never return your calls – the customer can call you back.
3 Put urgent enquiries at the bottom of the heap and let them gather dust.
4 Always interrupt customers who do get through. Better still, cut them off.
5 Be obnoxious and lose your temper – customers can be very irritating.
6 Free phone numbers are for wimps – use 0898 for all help lines.
7 Seal up all suggestion boxes and burn questionnaires as they're returned.
8 What questionnaires?

And remember

9 Always say 'have a nice day now' with a smarmy twang, to all your customers as they mutter away into the distance.

What follows is a whole series of ideas for opening up dialogue. Some we look at in more detail in the next chapter, but all of them are aimed at ways of opening up that relationship, building foundations, and helping you to actually start talking to customers.

And remember it isn't just the words you use that have an effect, it's the style of those words too.

Getting it right

So the important thing to ask yourself is:

How do we get customers to talk to us?

And also:

How do we get customers to continue to talk to us?

From dialogue to interactivity

One of the facets of the new way of looking at customers is working on language. So rather than simply thinking about dialogue, think also about interactivity. Interactivity implies listening and talking and a dialogue based on respect.

The problem with the traditional marketing approach of using hand-picked focus groups is a good example of why we need to move towards a more interactive model. Focus groups use hand-picked paid individuals who are given questions in an artificial setting. They do not really represent the marketplace.

Better to really get to know customers.

The following are just some ideas that may help:

1 You could set up a 24 hour helpline – a freephone number would be even better. Many companies are now investing in setting up better help facilities so that customers will actually make contact and come and talk to them. If you have ever tried to get through to one of the computer software helplines you will know just how frustrating it can be when there seems to be just one person for the whole of the country manning the helpline, and 10,000 people at any one time trying to get through.

So if you are going to have a helpline make sure it is properly and efficiently staffed. A three hour wait for advice on a minor computer breakdown is not guaranteed to develop a sense of relationship with that particular company.

2 Open up the building. You have already looked at how banks have done this, but it's worth asking yourself whether your building can seem more open to customers. Some companies have had open days to allow customers to come in and see what it's like. The key thing is that it needs to be planned, but if you can make your building more accessible and you can give people the chance to come in it's much more likely that you will be able to open up a dialogue with them, and an on-going dialogue at that.

The key to opening up the building is good signposting, access to back-of-house areas and of course a warm and friendly welcome.

But making your building less imposing is not the only way of making the face-to-face contact with customers feel more friendly and warm. One idea you may want to adopt is actually to get some of your staff to act as meeters and greeters.

Apparently a leading bank in Seattle has appointed such people. This is quite common in many restaurant chains who actually have certain staff ready to meet and greet customers. But why not apply this principle to other kinds of business? People after all like to be met and they like to be greeted in a friendly human way. If you can do this and surprise them, then you are clearly going to steal a march over the competition.

3 Leave clear answerphone messages explaining your opening hours. People need to know when they can come to you and when you are available, and this kind of thing can help.

4 Alternatively, ban answerphones if anyone is in the building. Insist that staff pick up the phone and talk, even if it isn't their phone that's ringing.

5 Establish contact names. The following example shows how not to do it.

'I received a nasty letter from my credit card company. I know they have got it wrong, because I had already sent my cheque off to pay the bill. But somehow, I had received a threatening letter from them. So I rang the number and explained the problem. The trouble was that at the bottom of the letter there was just an unintelligible squiggle that passed for a signature.

When I asked who I could speak to to complain, I was told I should write to the management. Facetiously, I asked "Is that capital T and capital M?" To which the uncomprehending person at the other end of the phone said "Yes".'

Don't do the kind of thing above. It's very important for people to know who they can contact, and to give out proper contact names. After all, it's the people behind these names who are going to be the foundation of any long-term relationship.

6 Try to give out short, clear and easy to complete questionnaires with every product you sell. People may not always fill them in but they are always a good source of information coming in from customers, and show that you take their suggestions seriously.

7 Direct dialling. Why not publicize direct dial names and numbers for your organization. One thing that frustrates people and puts them off talking to you is the feeling they will be passed from pillar to post. This has been a particular problem in the public sector, but it isn't only here that this is a problem. If you have ever tried to get through to a certain department in any large company to have a certain query answered, you may well have come across this kind of thing.

Derby City Council, for instance, recently set up direct dial numbers as a way of helping customers make contact quickly and easily, and making them feel confident that it is worth ringing up.

8 Get them to write to you. Send a freepost envelope or form with any correspondence that needs a response. Obviously this costs companies a bit more as they need to pay the Post Office in advance, but it's one sure-fire way of getting people to write back to you. After all, why should you expect them to spend their money to write to you to tell you things you need to know, and to help you develop your relationship with them.

9 Offer an incentive to the first number of customers to respond to you. For example women's magazines sometimes include free samples offers to get responses to questionnaires. This means you can actually split the cost between the magazine and the product manufacturer. But the point is people may need to be 'incentivized' in order to write to you, so you may need to offer a gift – we look at this in more detail in the next section.

10 The final thing with opening up your organization is to do what we call the Sumo Test. This is how it works.

The Sumo Test

One quick way to test if you really have a dialogue with your customers is to weigh your post bag.

How much mail do you receive each week? Can you lift up your mail bag single handed or do you need a sumo wrestler to help you?

It does not take a rocket scientist to tell you that a small post bag means your customers are not talking to you.

11 Don't insist that people only write to you. Allow people to make contact with you in whatever way they would like to – through the Internet, in person, by phone, by fax, and so on.

The important thing is to orientate the communication channels around the customers and the way they *want* to make contact with you.

Talking to customers overseas

Distance is not the only barrier to keeping in touch with customers overseas. Many countries have different expectations of service, products or behaviour.

Reputedly, the Japanese and Swedes are good listeners, whereas the French and Spaniards are not. Americans may expect a lively approach to customer relations – many fast food restaurants adopt a very familiar approach to their customers 'Hi, I'm Kelly and I'm your waitress for today'. The Germans may expect a more formal approach. Some cultures think it impolite to ask you to repeat something they don't understand; others will ask detailed technical questions until they are absolutely sure they understand.

These are generalizations, but they illustrate the need to communicate with your customer in a language and manner with which they are comfortable. Speak to your colleagues in the country you are dealing with and ask their advice.

Respect language differences

It's important if you are actually committed to getting people to make contact with you, that you don't put them off because they can't speak to you in their language. The English are notoriously bad at speaking other people's languages. Anyone who has lived overseas will know this is something of an international joke. However, it is important to really make an effort, if you are committed to an on-going relationship with customers, to actually speak their language.

SPEAKING IN TONGUES

Christies, the international auction house, asks every new employee to tell personnel what languages they speak. Hindi, Serbo Croat, Icelandic – the list is surprisingly diverse.

If customers want to speak in their mother tongue (ie not English), the personnel department check whether any member of staff speaks that language and calls them up to translate.

Sometimes it turns out that the customer can speak good English after all, but felt on principle that, as an international company, Christies should make the effort. Even if the resulting language is less than fluent, most customers usually greatly appreciate it.

This is a good example and it isn't just Christies that have employed it. Many local authorities have built up lists of people within the organization with different languages, so if someone wants to make contact, and hasn't got English as a language, someone will be able to talk to them and translate for them.

The following two examples show how companies have actively encouraged staff to talk to customers, and get customers to talk to them. In many ways you can see this talking as the foundation of an on-going relationship. After all, we have been exhorted recently:

'It's good to talk.'

Whatever you think of the advert, it is an important point, and it reinforces that keeping up an on-going, talking relationship with customers – where they feel happy to talk to you – is at the heart of actually getting your relationship right with them.

Getting it wrong

Not listening carefully to the customer can lead to some unfortunate conclusions and extreme penalties.

This is what happened to another company. You may not have such a grand example, but it is worth reminding yourself about your own department's horror stories.

THE RUNAWAY CITROEN

A few years ago a lady parked her Citroen on a slight incline and went to the shops. Not a great event, but it proved to be the start of a major consumer service row.

While she was away the car rolled down the hill crashing into another car. She was positive the handbrake had been on. It must have failed. The insurance company, however, refused to believe her.

Soon after a friend confided that she too had crashed her Citroen by leaving the handbrake off. A strange coincidence? The lady asked Citroen if there was a problem, only to receive a very curt reply saying she must have forgotten to put the handbrake on.

Incensed, the friends contacted Watchdog, the BBC consumer issues programme. The story created an avalanche of response. It emerged that several months earlier Citroen's engineers had discovered the brake problem. Some discs contracted on cooling, rendering the brakes useless if the car stood still for more than 20 minutes. Rather than recall every car, staff were warned to look out for this complaint and get senior staff to handle problems tactfully as they arose.

The employee who answered the lady's first enquiry did not listen to internal warnings or to the customer's problem. The result left Citroen looking very stupid, anti women drivers and with a large repair and damages bill.

On the other hand, putting it right even when it has gone wrong can have an enormously powerful impact.

'SORRY...'

The proprietor of a small soft furnishing firm ordered a pair of scissors, mail order. They were expensive because they were for trade work, and they were sold with the claim that they didn't break.

They broke. As soon as they arrived the buyer dropped them on a stone floor and the handle came off. Now, she felt a little uneasy – after all, she had dropped them on a very hard surface. But she rang anyway, to see what they said.

They said, 'Sorry'. Not, 'Sorry but there's nothing we can do,' but, 'Sorry, they shouldn't have broken.'

They said they would send a replacement pair first class post that day, without waiting for any proof of the break, and could the customer please return the original pair at her leisure.

The replacements arrived the following morning. The soft furnishing maker now spends a lot of money every year with a firm she feels trusts her, believes her and has always listened to her – a firm that sold her something that went wrong.

Writing to customers

This is the final section in this chapter, and is an area which is often overlooked.

Many companies spend lots of money and lots of time in training their staff to answer the phone in a friendly way, and writing customer-friendly marketing material, and putting together friendly adverts. However, the one area they often forget is letters, and you do so at your peril.

Organizations send out millions of letters every day to customers, and these letters create a clear impression of the company, and either do or don't encourage customers to make contact with that company, or start developing a relationship with it.

It can create very mixed signals if a company is very friendly in all respects, but then resorts to jargon and lack of clarity in its letters. Bad letters will always get people's backs up. A sticky part in a face-to-face conversation between staff and customer can be overcome during the course of the conversation. A badly received letter is badly received. It's there in black and white. And it's almost guaranteed to generate an angry phone call, or worse still, a mental note from the customer to go elsewhere next time.

The time spent working on a style of letter that reflects the way you actually want to be, is time well spent.

Modern companies who respect their customers will do all the following things with their letters:

- write them clearly. Any company that doesn't switch to plain English is stuck in the dark ages and is guilty of not showing respect to customers
- write them in a direct, personal voice – there will be liberal use of the words 'you' and 'we' and 'I'. People reading the letter will know who is writing it, why they are writing it, and what's expected of them
- write letters that sound as if they are written by a human being rather than generated by a computer and then churned out
- be clear about the voice the company wants to put across in the letters. Avoid the voice of the bureaucrat at all costs. Try to write more in the way that you would speak to customers on the phone or face to face.

How many times have you been contacted by your bank, solicitor or perhaps the Council and not had the faintest clue what they were trying to tell you? Corporate gobbledygook is something everyone loves to hate but it is a hard habit to break.

You don't need to use complex official language for a communication to be taken seriously. Try to use plain English, not jargon. Write clearly and say what you mean.

The same applies to the spoken word. The 15th century German church leader, Martin Luther, was renowned for preaching his sermons in the local dialect of the area he was visiting. Educated scholars could read his writings in printed pamphlets; the majority of people he preached to were illiterate. So Luther made a point of explaining his beliefs in familiar words they could understand.

It's just as true today. Expressing yourself clearly is particularly important when dealing with foreign markets as the following example shows :

BROKEN ENGLISH

Rolls Royce recently found a successful make of engine inexplicably began to break down, but only in certain countries. The product was technically sound. Qualified engineers had made thorough presentations to the new owners and the operating and service manuals covered everything. The problem became so serious that Rolls Royce sent teams of engineers out to each country affected, to no avail.

Finally they called in a specialist in cross-cultural matters who got to the root of the problem. The engines had failed in countries where the standard of English comprehension was insufficient to absorb instruction delivered in idiomatic English leaving the customer confused and helpless.

'I am a person not a number'

Official corporate language has a habit of dehumanising the customer. The last thing a company needs when trying to get to know their customer better and stay in touch.

Companies approaching the customer in this way need to refocus their language. Any communication should reflect the company's wish to build a positive and lasting relationship with the customer. This can work even when demanding payment on overdue bills.

TSB: A ROLE MODEL OF GOOD PRACTICE

The TSB approach is a true role model and something everyone can learn from.

One day the TSB received a letter from a very irate customer. He was complaining about a letter written in Bank-speak about a minor unintentional overdraft. He had been a customer for 30 years, never been overdrawn before and objected strongly to the letter. In his letter to TSB he wrote: *You wouldn't talk to me in this way, so why write to me like this.*

Rather than write a quick letter back, but essentially ignore the customer's complaint, TSB took this suggestion to heart.

They decided to look again at all their customer letters and rewrite them so they were clear, consistent and friendly, but firm when necessary.

Above all the new letters aimed to be free of corporate Bank-speak and write to customers in modern-day language.

The new letters are clear and approachable and use I and We and have stripped away words like 'advise' and 'facility'. In the new letters the communication is friendly and conducted as with an equal.

The exclusive treatment

The wrong attitude can come across in the simplest terms. Take the following letter from an exclusive country hotel, confirming a booking with the customer:

'Thank you for your reservation. I have much pleasure in confirming that we have reserved a double room for ...

Guests are respectfully reminded that any reservation made, whether verbal or written, forms a binding contract. We regret that should a cancellation be received within seven days of arrival a fee may be imposed at the discretion of the Management.

I trust the above meets with your approval.'

The customer is now ready to arrive, solicitor in tow, itching for a confrontation. The receptionist's original reply to the customer's enquiry had been friendly and informative. The Assistant Manager's confirmation of the booking undid all the receptionist's good work.

So it's absolutely important that in these letters you are actually creating a voice. And this means ironing out jargon, using short sentences, and, if you need to, using headings so people can find their way around a letter, plus actually understanding that a lot of people have low reading ages, so you need to speak to them in a voice, and using language, that they are likely to understand.

Using the language

Many companies refer to their customers using a not altogether complimentary language. The following are just some of the words companies use in their letters and other communications to refer to customers, which tend to dehumanise them:

buyer	vendee	vendor
patron	hirer	lessee
client	purchaser	farepayer
ratepayer	tourist	householder
passenger	debtor	creditor.

The message here is that customers are your customers, and they are human beings. So try to develop a discourse that reflects this. Try to use customer-friendly words, and words that make it clear that you treat your people as individuals. Make sure you write in this warm and human voice.

The round up

■ ■ ■

In this chapter we have looked at developing dialogues with customers.

If you aren't spending time doing this then the chances are you are going to have some unhappy customers.

At the heart of this are two things:

- making your organization and department accessible to customers
- developing a letters-style that talks person-to-person with customers.

To test how well you are doing try calling into your department and posing as a customer. See how easy it is to make contact. Also check out your letters and see if you have drifted into using company-speak.

7

Broadening your relationship with customers

In chapter six you looked at ways of keeping in touch with customers, and opening up channels of communication. You also looked in chapter five at the importance of your staff keeping customers contented.

In this section you are going to start to look at ways of broadening the relationship you have with your customers. Some may be appropriate to you, some may not. Some your organization may already employ, some your organization may not. The important thing in this chapter is to feel free to mix and match, and choose the ideas that will help you keep your customers for life.

The emphasis in this chapter is that customers are there to be won and kept. Some companies have a kind of 'holiday fling' type of approach to customers. They may well excite them briefly or attract them, but the magic soon falls off under the impact of distance. Successful organizations overcome the distance between themselves and customers by helping customers to feel part of the team, or feel a great loyalty towards that company. In some more extreme examples, companies have started working in partnership with their customers, so the two are inextricably linked.

We can see the relationship challenge as a kind of company/customer magic bridge. If you can get the relationship working then you have a bridge both you as a manager and the customer can cross.

Like all bridges, it will need maintenance and attention and sometimes, even, structural work. You may even find that you need to design a new bridge if the old one is no longer good enough.

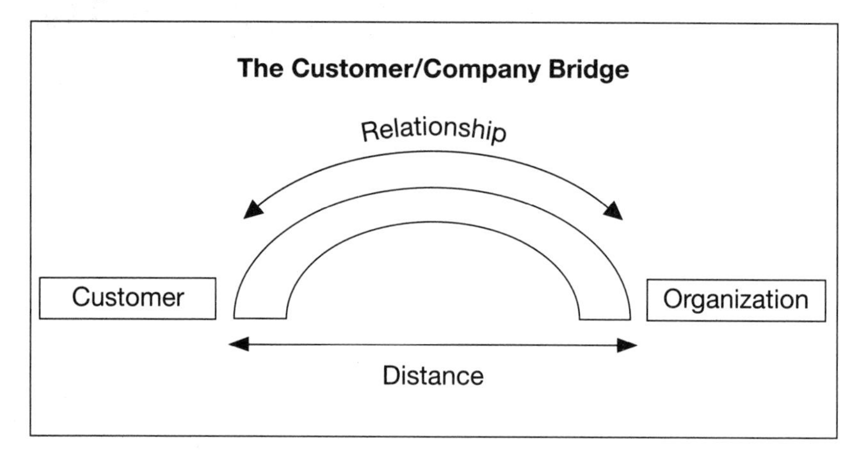

You can see the following chapter as a menu from which to choose. Each option is there to help you build the all-important bridge.

Each section within it gives you new examples and new ideas about how to broaden your relationship with customers.

Show you are serious

This is important and very much ties in with the holiday fling metaphor above. People enter into holiday flings not believing they will be serious. They are fun but not designed to last. They usually don't turn out to be serious. However, successful companies show they are serious about getting to know their customers, stay in contact with them, and listen to what they have to say. Customers soon get tired of taking part in a relationship if it seems unequal.

So you are aiming for a serious relationship built upon equality. If you make a complaint for instance, and the company ignores it, it's unlikely you will make a complaint again.

Sainsbury have taken customers' complaints to heart with a £20m campaign to take the agony out of the supermarket aisles. Better trolleys, extra peak-time packers and free nappies in the baby changing room – all trumpeted by a major advertising campaign. Part of the campaign features video box interviews with customers saying what they want from shopping at Sainsbury. The ultimate evidence of listening seriously to your customers.

Move on to a customer's territory

■ ■ ■

One way of showing a commitment to developing a relationship with customers is to move on to their territory. This is important because customers often feel at a great disadvantage and it's important to realize that as with any relationships, the best relationships are those that are based on equality rather than dominance. Some organizations have grasped this nettle and decided to go out and meet customers on their own territory in order that the odds seem a little more equal.

This has often been true in the public sector in recent years as organizations have made the decision to go out and discover what customers want in the places where they live, rather than insisting the customer write in for instance. So most local authorities these days will at least have some inclination to get out of their offices and go to the customer's environment to talk to them.

Examples of moves on to customer's territory include:

- mobile benefit buses
- neighbourhood offices
- local and regular liaison meetings.

These are all designed to take the service provider to the people – to narrow the gap between the parties. And it isn't only the public sector that can learn from this. Everyone needs to get closer to the public.

Do the following test

- *Do customers always have to come to you?*
- *Do they always have to come to you during normal working hours?*
- *Do you provide any mobile services?*
- *Have you ever discussed getting out and meeting customers?*
- *Do you run any liaison or interest groups?*

If you answered yes to the first two questions and no to the remaining three it looks very much as though you are conducting your business on your own territory.

156 Helping people with special needs

Most of us find it hard to really understand the requirements of special needs groups. When it comes to improving facilities for people with impaired vision or hearing, the elderly or those with mobility problems (all of whom are customers) many organizations fall short. Some useful lessons can be learnt from the charitable sector which has consistently attempted to facilitate the involvement of disabled people and move on to a more equal footing with them.

WHAT THE CUSTOMER REALLY WANTS

SHAPE is a charitable organization which works to improve facilities for the disabled. Their funds are limited, but their determination to give their customers what they not only want but need is immense.

A new Regional Arts Officer for SHAPE was asked to produce a policy document outlining all the desired improvements to arts facilities in her region. A huge task. The officer was new to the area. So rather than rely on internal reports she decided to ask the customers themselves, those with special needs.

She arranged visits to every venue in the region. Meetings

coincided with gatherings of special needs groups – Derby & Joan club afternoons, occupational therapy groups, an editorial meeting of the local newspaper for the blind.

A month of travelling and talking to the customers resulted in a thorough policy paper that clearly stated what the customers needed.

But it isn't just charities that have made the effort to shift on to people's territory and find out what they want.

The following example shows how the managers at one bus company in Belfast took the time and effort to get out of their offices and get in to the local environment, to really find out, and show they were committed to customer needs. The results made the effort well worthwhile.

EUROPA BUS CENTRE

Belfast's Europa Bus Centre is a true answer to the customer's prayers. Ulsterbus conducted a survey of their customers to find out what they wanted, what really annoyed them and what the company could do to improve things.

Most complaints said the station was cold, unwelcoming, dirty and generally a nasty place to wait. Exactly what you have to do for a bus!

Ulsterbus's response was the Europa Bus Centre. A bright high-tech terminus with a cafe, shop, comfortable seats and airport style departure screens. District Manager Richard Hudson explains:

> *'It is the first depot we have built in this style and it shows our commitment to our customers. We brought everybody indoors, there's lots of information, a heated waiting room and all that sort of stuff. It's more customer friendly.'*

This approach has been good for business. Passenger numbers are increasing. Extra income has also come from selling the shop and cafe franchises and through new car parks, enabling Ulsterbus to run a park and ride scheme.

So you should:

- look to get out of the office and into the community as much as you can
- help people to take part
- always look to get away from the *we have power you are just customers* mentality.

Putting the fun into a business relationship

Another idea that some companies have explored is that of putting on a 'fun day'. They are a useful way of helping people feel more at ease with the organization, and allow the organization to move on to their territory. Supermarkets for instance now sometimes hold family days with face painting, clowns and a couple of staff dressed up as Ninja turtles, for example. This is good because it attracts children, and along with the children come the adults. When you have got the adults, you can use the time with them to do things like test products, and even sell products too.

In the public sector the idea of a fun day has been an important way for large organizations like Housing Action Trusts making contact with their communities' home ground.

For instance, Stonebridge Housing Action Trust in West London is currently organizing a major sports and fun day. This will include cricket matches, stalls and various events to try to attract the whole community. With the whole community together, staff will then go out and make themselves visible, and start speaking to the community about how they want their estate to be developed. It's the fun and sports day that allows the estate to feel that the organization cares about it and is prepared to meet them on their own territory. It is this partnership approach to customers that allows a long-term relationship to build up.

This is, of course, very important with the Housing Action Trusts, whose sole aim is to work with the community to develop run down estates. You can't do this without an on-going partnership and an on-going relationship. You can't find out what people want from their homes in 20 years time by a quick bit of market research. Instead, to make this kind of activity work, you need to develop deep links with the community, and meet the community on their own grounds. This might mean, for instance, turning up to local bingo and social clubs that already exist. In other words, you can plug into the existing infrastructure of the estate and then find out what people want.

Although this kind of approach is being pioneered in HATs like Stonebridge, it's a model that can easily be applied to the private sector as well. Just stop and ask yourself when was the last time you truly got out of the office and met your customers on their own territories. Also, think to yourself what effect this would have on them. They may in fact at the start be mistrustful, or fall over in shock.

However, if you demonstrate you want to build up a more ongoing approach by meeting them on their ground, the chances are you are likely to have much more success than by just sending out the odd form or questionnaire, and waiting for the responses.

Using the faithful postal questionnaire

■ ■ ■

Although the last paragraph might seem to denigrate the humble questionnaire, it can be a useful way of developing relationships with people.

The main problem with postal questionnaires is the time they take to complete. A loyal customer is more likely to take the trouble. They already like what your company does, so they have a vested interest in improving the service you give them. Asking people what they want can also work to attract new custom. A carefully structured postal questionnaire can provide a great deal of information which helps to improve your relationship with your customer.

'VOTE FOR ME – I'M INTERESTED IN YOUR OPINION'

Twickenham is a marginal Tory seat with a Liberal Democrat Council. Twickenham Liberal Democrats sent a new resident a freepost questionnaire with the following letter :

> *You appear from the electoral register to be voting in this constituency for the first time. According to local surveys the Liberal Democrat run Council receives strong support from local people. I am writing to ask for your views on the issues which concern you.*

A simple tick box questionnaire was enclosed together with a copy of the Liberal Democrat newsletter. Along with the letter came a personalized letter with the words:

> *This is just one of the ways we regularly keep in touch with what you have to say.*

So what makes a good questionnaire?

The following is a very rough guide:

1 ***Keep it relevant.*** You need to be sure what you want to find out from your questionnaire, rather than just find out any old information and then see what's interesting.

2 ***Keep it short.*** People don't like filling in questionnaires, so keep them as short as possible and just stick to the relevant facts.

3 ***Ask concrete questions.*** It's no good asking questions that people find hard to answer or that you'll find difficult to process the answers to. Instead, ask questions you will be able to get useful information from, and information you can actually use.

An example of a bad questionnaire came recently from BT. The question asked was: '*Rank 1 – 5; does BT care about its customers?*'

This is an almost impossible question to answer for customers. The question arises 'what do you mean by care?'. And it is hard to see what the company would do with the answers it received. How could the responses possibly help in any concrete way to improve services. Instead it looks like a rather cynical attempt to get a 'feel good' response to a meaningless question that can then be rolled out as evidence of how wonderful the company is.

4 Produce a questionnaire that ***allows actual ideas to be generated***. In any questionnaire always add a section where people can write their own comments and suggestions.

5 ***Ask questions that allow you to compare data.*** On a questionnaire you need to ask questions that allow you to compare results over time and see where there are improvements or problems developing.

Staying in touch with customers

Providing aftercare services

Often new customers are not sure what they should be doing with their product, how to care for it or go about ordering new parts. The simplest form of instruction manual can sometimes seem mind boggling if it is the first time you have seen it.

Aftercare services can help you soothe the customer into the early stages of their relationship with you. An example of aftercare service is Porsche, who offer new Porsche owners special driving lessons on how to handle their new car. After all, driving a high performance car like a Porsche for the first time can be a dangerous business, and the company has a sense of social responsibility.

Here are some tips as to the sorts of services you can offer to make the customers' life easier.

The key to aftercare services is that they need to be:

- genuine
- helpful
- personal.

People don't want to be overcome with a whole welter of information. They want a meaningful aftercare service that adds value – not a gimmick to sell on some extras. They want the information they are likely to need .

Also the aftercare service is a chance to make contact with customers and cement that relationship.

The following is what American Express do when you take out a gold card. It shows the real value of aftercare services and the way they can help you sell products and cement a feeling of loyalty to your product.

Case study

AMERICAN EXPRESS

If you apply for an American Express gold card the card will arrive with a little sticker on it. The sticker reads 'Ring this number for your card to be validated'.

You phone the number and the person who answers checks that you are who you say you are, and validates the card. However, it doesn't end here. The person will then run through the benefits of the card, and how to use it. He or she will also take this as an opportunity to briefly describe some of the other services American Express offer. These include things like holiday insurance, and a range of other free services to customers.

One of the most interesting and useful free services they offer is a travel service. American Express give you a number, and the travel service allows you, if you have travel arrangements, to simply say where you want to get to, what time you want to get there, and whether you want to stay overnight. The travel service will then book hotels and make reservations for you. This is an extraordinarily good aftersales service.

For a start it offers people a range of products they are likely to actually want to buy.

Secondly, it puts a voice and a name to what is otherwise an impersonal piece of plastic. You have a contact who takes time to talk to you about what you want from your card and how they can help.

Thirdly, they are able to offer things the customer actually wants. You can use this opportunity to buy, for instance, car protection.

Fourthly, American Express are able to offer a very useful free service, which most people take advantage of. At the end of the conversation, always with a very pleasant person, you feel part of the American Express gold card ethos. It feels like your card, and the company feels much more human.

The chances are you will then use that card much more than any other cards in your purse or wallet.

The example above encapsulates the essence of effective aftercare. It is personable and useful and feels genuine. It also says 'welcome to our club'.

Something to do

First what aftercare do you offer?

If none, then you've a way to go. If you do provide aftercare how does it rank from 1 – 5 against the criteria of:

- genuine
- helpful
- personal.

Direct mail

Direct mail is suffering a personality crisis. Much of it is dismissed as junk mail, cluttering up post boxes and showering out of our Sunday newspapers.

When used with care it can be a useful tool for keeping in touch with distant customers – but handle it with care.

The concept is an old one, originating in an English gardening catalogue in 1667. Direct mail is based on a standard letter or leaflet sent to a list of customers selected from the company's files or gathered from a complementary source, all of whom seem to be interested in a particular offer the company has to make. The key to direct mail is that the letter needs to be personalized, so that it seems relevant to the person who receives it. Obviously, though, this is very difficult when you are mailing out to large numbers of people.

Today, most of us are familiar with direct mail from charities and mail order companies. The problem with it is that it can often be a very blunt weapon. By its nature it's targeted at customers who all seem to have a particular interest. The problem with direct mail is that it feels a rather one-way method of communication, and after all relationships are based on two-way communication. If your letter simply tells people about yourself that doesn't seem the basis for much of a relationship.

The other problem that can happen with direct mail is that individuals can receive large quantities of it and so become jaded, or indeed receive a warning letter from a bank for instance, and then a direct mail offering further credit cards. These things can tend to degrade the whole relationship between customer and company, so direct mail needs to be used with care.

Mail order

While talking about this kind of thing, it's interesting to know that mail order is starting to make a comeback. Many High Street fashion shops like NEXT found that they were in direct competition from the improved quality catalogue outlets, such as Freemans. They now actively encourage mail order as a sideline. And it isn't just NEXT that have done this. The top quality kitchen and cook shop, Divertimenti, has also gone down this road.

The advantage of mail order is that it may open up new markets for you and it can feel like quite a personal relationship. People actually look forward to receiving their goods from direct mail and it can allow you to open up different ways for them to pay for the products. Also with mail order people have to write to you, and this business of getting people to make contact with a company is one of the foundation stones for any relationship.

More about the telephones

You have already looked in part at some of the benefits of telephones in terms of customer relationships in the previous chapter, but here we will look at them in more detail, and stress just how important they are. Remember, when you pick up a telephone you can talk to half a billion people in 186 different countries. Literally, the telephone puts you in contact with the world, and companies who ignore it do so at their peril.

Done well and used effectively and simply, the telephone can perhaps be one of the quickest and easiest ways of building a relationship with your customer. However, people do feel very sensitive about their personal space, and can feel intruded upon if you ring them in an inappropriate way or at an inappropriate moment. However, sometimes using the phone can be a nice way of cementing that all-important customer relationship. Take the following example.

BT follow up repairs with a simple phone call asking questions like whether the engineer arrived on time, whether the equipment has been properly repaired, and whether the engineer cleared up afterwards. This simple use of the telephone, targeted at the right time in the relationship, is very useful and can be used as an important way of improving customer loyalty.

GWYNNE PRINT

Gwynne Print have the 'keeping in touch' call as the cornerstone of the way their organization handles customers. People from the company will make calls for instance announcing an opening party for a new print works, checking that customers are satisfied with their service, and so on.

It's the Gwynne Print philosophy that no problem is too small and that the phone is one of the main ways of keeping in with a friendly contact. It's a way of keeping in touch, even when people move on to a different company. In many ways we can see this as a kind of hospitality angle, because one of the important aspects of making telephone calls is that it is social, and it is interactive.

Many people find telemarketing highly intrusive. Anyone with any sense hangs up immediately on any double-glazing salesman but a follow up call asking if you are happy with a service you have been given is very important, and is normally liked by customers.

It's the kind of thing that with a bit of training and some guidance from you, your team can start at once to make an immediate impact.

MELBOURNE CITY COUNCIL

Melbourne City Council found from customer comments that they had a problem with their in-house work contracting. People were frightened of answering the door as they weren't sure whether people were bogus or real workmen, and there was a problem in that workmen tended not to want to talk to customers.

The council instigated a programme where the workmen doing the job would phone the customer first of all to tell them they were on their way and to confirm they would be bringing council identification. When they had completed the job they either knocked on the door to talk the job through with the customer, or if the customer wasn't there would phone later on that day to confirm they had done the job, and see whether there were any remaining problems. They used the phone in this way to cement individual, one-on-one relationships between junior and middle ranking staff and the community they served.

Answerphones revisited

It sounds simple and it is – answering machines are a great help if there is no-one in the office. It's important not to rely on them and switch them on if you don't want to talk to customers, but it's better to have an answerphone and get a message rather than lose the customer altogether.

There are now new style answerphones which will rerecord your message if you are not happy with it to stop the 'Oh no, I hate talking to machines and I've forgotten what to say,' panic reaction.

Phone plus

There are other innovations and uses of the phone in terms of building and broadening customer relationships.

The following are just some of them:

1 ***Phone banking.*** This is a recent development but it's one important way of helping customers use the service in a way they find convenient. Banks like TSB have recently launched a highly-successful Phone bank, and these things are seen to show a commitment to the kind of services a customer wants.

2 ***DirectLine insurance.*** You can now phone DirectLine with details of your claim. You don't even have to fill in a form. This is a brilliant example of actually using the phone as an on-going tool rather than simply as a one-off communication device.

3 ***Touch tone telephones.*** Many companies are now using touch tone phones to help people select products or bypass some of the problems of switchboards. When you ring up many companies, you may well get a message asking you what kind of problem you have, or what service you want, and then telling you which button on your phone to push in order to get through to exactly the right person in the organization.

4 ***Special information lines.*** You can offer a dedicated number where customers actually get advice.

For instance Persil offer their Careline, which is an 0800 number. On the one hand this will help you to cross sell, but it will also help to build up data on a customer. A Careline is also a good way of picking up any mild dissatisfaction or complaints people have and handling them quickly and responsibly.

Regis McKenna in his article 'Real Time Marketing'* points out the folly of simply using 0800 numbers (and indeed the Internet) as one-way communication channels – from you to customers. Instead he says you should use them as genuine two-way communications – listening posts as well as microphones. He believes we should think dialogue not broadcast.

Try stamping all your products with an 0800 number. Kellogg's has begun to place an 0800 number on the inside top of its cereal packets.

* July/August 1995 issue of the *Harvard Business Review*.

5 ***Single contact lines.*** You can also offer a single contact line, so if a customer wants specialist advice they can ring you. For instance Dyfed Fire Service offers a Fire Prevention Officer on call at any time. The number is widely publicized, so if you ring that number you will get through to a Fire Prevention Officer.

And finally, when it comes to telephones, the important thing is to get the right number to customers. Don't be shy. Make sure everyone knows your number and particularly all your customers.

Centre One Tax Office, which is the largest Inland Revenue office in the UK, has produced a wall chart which displays all the relevant numbers for different queries. This means that people know exactly who to ring. If you do this though beware, because the chances are when you start publicizing how to get through people will take you at your word and phone. This means calls will increase and you may need to increase the number of staff to handle them.

But exercising the option of not publicising your phone number is a bad one because customers won't make contact with you, and as we have seen time and time again, if they don't make contact with you there is no relationship.

If a wall chart with contact numbers on is too large why not produce a simple laminated card or even put the number on a bottle top.

Try anything, as long as people know how to get hold of you.

Try the simple 1, 2, 3 phone test

Ask yourself:

- *If I were a customer and I didn't have the phone number of this department, how easy would it be to get hold of it?*
- *How long would it take to get through when I got the phone number?*
- *How could I find out the name of the person I needed to talk to?*

Remember you can't buy loyalty

One response companies and departments often have to winning and keeping customers is to offer discounted products. They figure that if they do so, then they will be able to almost buy a customer's loyalty.

However, this type of price promotion often simply doesn't work. There are a number of reasons against cutting prices and offering price promotions.

These are:

- they can distort the sales volume. Cutting the price may lead to higher turnover and higher sales, but there is no link between this and higher profits
- you can attract defectors. You may well increase trade in the short term, as people try your product, but as soon as the promotion is over they may well defect back to their traditional products
- you can annoy existing customers. Customers often feel angry if they have paid the full price for a product, only to find shortly after that there is a price promotion on the way.

What can also happen is that people start to lose faith in your pricing and simply hang on, waiting for the inevitable sale to come along. The following is an example of how price promotions can really annoy customers.

SAAB

One of the authors of this book recently bought a new Saab motor car. It was a high-value product, and he had to wait eight weeks for the car to be delivered. Two weeks after delivery, a letter arrived from the dealer. This was the first communication he had received since he bought the car. He didn't have a phone call to see if he was enjoying driving the car, or whether he had any problems, or whether there was anything else the dealer could do. This letter announced that there was a new price promotion on Saab cars, and the very model he had paid a reasonable sum of money for was now available for £2,000 less.

This price promotion did not please this customer, and has made him think very carefully about whether he will buy another Saab in the future.

The point is that you want loyal customers to value your company for the quality it offers and, of course, the service.

Obviously people do think about price, but as you saw in the first chapter in this book, price is only one element in the complex business of finding out what customers want. So, if you do decide to have a crazy sale be careful, and be clear about why you are doing it, and of course be aware of some of the dangers in terms of developing a relationship with customers.

Using the leading edge

There are whole range of examples of leading edge technologies and the like that can help you to broaden your ties with customers.

All companies can do with the helping hand of technology, and many companies are finding ways of putting new technology to use in terms of building up the on-going relationship with customers, and developing that relationship. In fact, new technology is offering a whole new way of bringing companies closer to customers, and allowing companies to keep customers up to date with what they are offering. Building a positive relationship with customers who aren't on your doorstep can be very time-consuming, and this is one of the ways that new technology can step in to decrease that distance. The following are some ideas:

Databases

Databases are in some ways the shape of things to come. Although they have been around for some time, people are only now starting to get the full potential use out of them. Databases can be a major tool in the on-going business of keeping in contact with customers.

The databases we are talking about are essentially a massive detective agency within just a few microchips. Databases allow a company to market their services or products to individuals rather than a nebulous mass of the population, and this of course avoids that unfortunate scatter-gun effect that can often be the result of TV advertising and the like.

There are challenges though, when using databases. The main one is to make them economically viable. They cost a lot of money to design and maintain, and they also take up a lot of time, and in some ways the rewards can be quite intangible. In favour of them though, is they do allow you to keep in touch with a large number of customers.

Many companies now have databases, and these can act as a very quick way of helping people stay in contact. In the old days, there was nothing worse than ringing up and someone saying 'Hang on a minute, I have got to find your records'. You would then hear a frantic rooting around in files and sifting through piles of paper, and the odd swear word or two as it became clear that your file had gone missing. There is no excuse for this now. If one of your customers calls up, you should be able to get all their details on screen as soon as their call comes in.

This allows you to know what you are talking about, and can give you some useful ways of knowing what your customers do and don't like. Some of the best hotel chains, like The Savoy and The Ritz always knew the likes and dislikes of their specific customers.

But the new relationship databases allow that personal touch much more easily. So it may be that you record details like you don't put flowers in a guest room if they suffer from hay fever. The use of these more relationship type databases allows businesses to be much more responsive, and actually know what it is people do and don't like.

Of course, there is an issue of confidentiality. Sometimes companies can collect confidential information. Indeed, nothing will annoy a customer more than thinking that their details have become part of a massive database which will then spew out letters at every turn. So it's important to take a leaf from what the charities have done. In other words, people's addresses are confidential, and have not been used by mass appeal mailings. The idea is that they won't do something that would jeopardize a relationship.

You have only got to look at the way airlines and hotels use their databases to actually make specific offers, to see just how effective they can be.

DATABASES

British Airways have developed an executive club for frequent fliers. Frequent fliers carry a card. When they get to check-in, the BA staff member swipes the card and this reveals important details like the person's favourite seats, and any dietary requirements. Also the database shows how often and where these people have flown on previous flights. This then will indicate how aware they are of what it is like at their particular destination. If it is a new destination, staff can offer these customers assistance and information. If it's familiar, this can be acknowledged and people are just left to get on with it.

Other companies too are using databases in this way. One of the best examples is the hotel chains. Marriott Hotels, for instance, have a computer system that allows receptionists to know as the customer checks in whether he or she wants an iron in their room, whether they prefer a non-smoking room, what floor they prefer, or whether the bill will be settled by the customer, or the firm.

This kind of information allows front-line staff to really know what customers are after, and offer an excellent service.

Discretion is important though. People will become very unhappy if they feel their information on a database is being passed on to companies without their permission. Customers may well want to hunt out the source of any junk mail or other enquiry that comes as a result of them being on a database.

There are also systems such as CMT that will allow you to tap into market research on millions of households in the UK alone. The information is organized around hundreds of lifestyle and purchasing details. For instance the system will give you details of ABC groups, social habits, product consumption, earning and financial arrangements for different people.

You can use this to back up your hypotheses as to what your customers are looking for. Also on the agenda are relationship databases. These are being used, for instance, to personalize company communications to customers.

But databases are not just a way of finding out information, they can be used for a whole variety of other things too. For instance Levi Strauss offer a made-to-order service for its jeans. People's details are logged into a database and the jeans manufactured individually for $10 more than the normal price. The information is stored on database and can be used when new products become available. The database is used as a way of customizing a service.

We can see this as a kind of virtual intimacy.

Use software for customers

Federal Express gives its customers specially designed software and computer terminals so they can track the delivery of their parcels. It provides real-time information for customers. And here lies one of the main uses of new technology. It allows you to be in touch quickly with up-to-date information.

Use the fax

There are now over 25 million fax machines in Europe. Fax machines give you the advantage of being able to produce things like instant newsletters, and updates on latest offers. They also give you the chance to offer instant response ordering for your goods.

A fax is a quick route into people's offices and businesses. A fax is also somehow more difficult to ignore than a simple phone call.

So, why not use the fax to make contact with customers? On the one hand it may offer a nice surprise, and on the other it can give you the opportunity to have fun.

People are quite happy to receive jokey and light fax messages – much more than similar phone calls.

Home computers

Many, many people now have computers at home, and this has allowed companies to start providing a much more personal service to customers without the customer even having to leave home.

Barclays Bank, for instance, will be the first of the Big Four clearing banks to introduce an electronic home banking service, which will be available to its ten million customers. The system, which was developed in association with Visa, means that customers can pay bills, update their statements, and transfer cash using the Microsoft Windows system from the comfort of their own home.

Of course, there have been dissenting voices, and some people have feared that hackers will take off with their hard earned cash. However the bank have developed special encryption techniques to curb this risk. Barclays expect the system, which will be piloted by over 2,000 customers in the autumn of 1995, to become the norm for the future.

There are a whole range of other companies offering services at home, and this business of actually providing a service in the home is one important way to show that you care enough about customers to provide them with a service that meets their changing needs. The spread of computer based services is likely to be enormous in the next few years.

You might be able to think of ways you can offer some of your services in the home to people via their computers.

The Internet

The Internet is now a worldwide system of communication. Businesses across the land are now putting details about their services on the Internet.

It's no longer just crusty academics or computer-weirdoes who have access to it. People of all ages, and in all parts of the world, are now plugging into the Internet, and you need to make sure that, if possible, your company is represented.

An example of just how swift the Internet can be is that Greenpeace logged a report, their first, when they were being stormed by French commandos.

Has your company thought about putting some pages on the Internet? If not, why not? The Internet is important because it shows you are bang up to date with modern advances in information, and may open up a whole range of new communication possibilities with your customers.

The most important use of the Internet is not that you can use it to *tell* people about yourself, but that you can use it to *communicate*. For instance:

THE BBC AND THE NET

The BBC are now increasingly opening up access to listeners and viewers by the Internet. One BBC programme producer guarantees to spend three hours a week responding to queries about his programme on the Internet. He claims that this is the future for the BBC because it will lead to a much more democratic system of customer feedback.

e-mail

Many companies now have e-mail and often this can be used to broaden and deepen the dialogue and relationship with customers.

Microsoft have recently used e-mail to develop new products. They have made available new products to a range of different customers, and then invited them to give their comments via e-mail. Microsoft claim that they have been able to take on over 20,000 separate comments about new products which have then gone directly into improving them before they have gone onto the main market.

Interactive TV

Book into a Forte hotel and you will find an interactive TV in your room. You can use this TV to arrange your checkout, order room service, and find out information about the hotel.

Back to some simple tools

Saying sorry is simple

Among all the high-tech and innovative new ways of looking at how to develop a relationship with customers, it's important not to lose touch with some of the simple things that some of the successful customer relationships are built upon.

One of the most basic things that companies should do is not to be afraid to apologize.

Simply saying sorry can do a great deal to alleviate a difficult situation, especially if the customer expects, or is looking for, an argument. For instance, if they come in and return faulty goods, and you can almost preempt their anger and diffuse the situation, the chances are they will buy more goods from you. They don't remember the things that went wrong, but they do remember how you actually dealt with it. So, getting an apology from the manager before the customer demands it can make all the difference.

It shows them that their problem is being taken seriously, and that you respect them enough to listen to them. Often this simple apology can be very appropriate, and can definitely help develop a relationship.

It's important, though, not to overdo things. The manager in Monty Python's restaurant sketch is perhaps a bit extreme. He starts by humbly and sincerely apologizing for the inconvenience caused to his customers, but finally breaks down uncontrollably, unable to face the horrors of failure, and kills himself … and all over just a dirty fork!

So, the important thing is to be aware that saying sorry is not a shameful activity. It doesn't mean you are grovelling or you are reflecting badly on your organization. Instead, saying sorry is a way of starting a relationship afresh with a customer, and helping them feel able to come back to you again.

Swift recall procedures

Of course you may well need to put in place a recall procedure. If a persistent problem arises, you may need to write to customers and recall the goods, even if their particular goods have not failed as yet. This of course is common sense, and many car manufacturers have asked customers to bring cars in to be checked when they have found there is a fault.

When customers say good-bye: exit interviews

As well as this, you need to think about how you actually go about converting the leaving customer. In other words, all may well not be lost, even though they say they are going to leave you. It's important that if customers are thinking of, or indeed are, leaving, you should ask them why. Even if the customer still decides to walk away and not use your service again, you should learn something about how to improve the service for the future.

In many ways customers who are planning not to come back are often the most honest. The chances are they will tell you if you ask them exactly what you didn't do right and why they have decided to go to one of your competitors.

Many companies use exit interviews in order to get this useful feedback, and show that they are still interested in customers, and believe there may still be mileage in the relationship.

For instance the Royal Society for the Protection of Birds called all its members who wanted to resign after a controversial TV documentary. They took time to find out why their members were angry and listen to their complaints. In the event, and because of these exit interviews, more than half the number who earlier said they were going to resign decided to reinstate their membership. It's important though, with exit interviews, not to bully the customer.

There's no point in phoning them and haranguing them about

why they have decided to leave your wonderful organization. Bullying doesn't work. Customers simply won't respond.

Treat everything you do as an advert

There are other things you can do to try and show customers that you are interested in them, and develop the relationship. One important thing is that everything you do is an advert for your company, and this goes right throughout the company.

Everything your staff do, whenever they are in the public eye, is an advert or anti-advert for your company.

'I DIDN'T RECOGNIZE YOU'

In a local branch of a national chain of estate agents, the receptionist had had a hard day. All the negotiators were out and she was carrying the can on her own. When someone walked in at one minute to five it was the last straw.

'We're closing now', she said, fairly curtly.

Now, you don't say things like that to the Personnel Director of your own firm ... if you know who they are. Fortunately for her, the firm took this as a sign that their training needed sharpening up, instead of writing it off as an individual blip. The receptionist went on the course, instead of the dole.

Many companies that use delivery vans have realized this same syndrome. It's all well and good feeling that a shop is fine and the staff are friendly, but if you get cut up by one of their lorries on the motorway, or gestured at, or hooted, or have sexist comments shouted at you from a window, then this reflects very badly on the company.

Because delivery vans are so notorious, many companies have decided to address the problem. Dominos Pizzas received a number of complaints about the driving of their moped delivery service. Now you will find clearly positioned on all the mopeds a phone number and a comment that says 'If you don't like my driving, call this number'. Dominos aren't the only company to do this.

Many companies have now taken up the gauntlet, and put phone numbers on the sides of their vans. This means that you can ring up the company, and that they care about you.

More importantly, if you do ring to complain, it gives a personal relationship between you and the company employee, and allows them to put your mind at rest as a consumer.

Body Shop have taken this one step further, and they now use their delivery vans to advertise that company's charity campaign. For instance things like supporting Romanian orphans. They realize that vans are useful advertising space, and that everything we do is an advert.

So the important thing is make sure your staff are clear about the fact that everything is an advert, and that there are no confused messages given out. The following is a true story, and is based on one of the people interviewed when we were writing this book. They told us:

'I had a good example of these rather jagged service levels from BT. I spoke to a BT sales assistant who was helpful and charming, and who suggested a better and cheaper option for installing my phone. I was very pleased with this, and they really seemed to signal that they had my best interests at heart. Later in the day I rang up directory enquiries for a telephone number. I happened to be asking for someone who had a rather unusual name.

When I said the name the BT person said 'You must be joking. That's not a real name', and hung up. This really sent me confused messages as to BT's real attitudes to customers. I felt in a way there was no guarantee that I had been getting a good experience of BT. It may have been one bad apple, but this for me seemed to rot the whole cart.'

There are ways around the problem. There will of course be times when the customer is so infuriating that you and your staff will cheerfully want to strangle them. This is particularly true in high pressure front-line jobs. It's important to always use polite language, and to make the customer feel respected. This also can help front-line staff to control their temper, and to calm the whole situation down.

There are ways, too, of treating customers like family – making them feel really special, valued, and welcome – even loved. So, just as you may at times feel like strangling a close relative, so there is the option of giving something extra to customers, like you would to family.

The next chapter builds on this.

8

Doing that little bit extra

Establish appropriate relationships

Relationships have to be appropriate. The important thing is to be aware that different customers are looking for different things from a service, so you need to make sure that your staff realize that although everything is a shop window, an advert, they need to be quite subtle in the kind of service and the relationship they deliver.

Forte Post House realized this in their restaurants. After all, some people using a restaurant are business people looking to make a quick getaway and get to a meeting. Others are in on a leisure trip, or just for a romantic meal. Some may well not have been to a hotel restaurant at any point in their lives.

So Forte have trained staff to identify different kinds of customer, and offer different kinds of service based on their needs. So for business customers the service is efficient, prompt and professional. A business lunch is never interrupted by one of the serving staff coming over and asking how the meal was at an inappropriate moment. Business people are allowed to get on with their meal and with the minimum amount of fuss.

However, if staff identify that a customer seems not to have been to a hotel restaurant before, they will be offered lots of help and encouragement. The menu will be carefully explained, and throughout the meal the serving staff will visit to make sure everything is OK.

For a romantic dinner again, the service style needs to be unobtrusive and helpful.

Forte have undertaken a major analysis of all the kinds of customer, and are developing training around different customers. The message from the company is clear – customers want a relationship, but they want different kinds of relationship. Everything we do is an advert, but we need to advertise differently as it were to different people as we are serving them.

Using hospitality

In many ways, some people feel frightened about giving the red carpet treatment to customers. But hospitality really does work.

But why are people so suspicious of it? For a start people are very confused about the limits of hospitality. They sometimes think that hospitality is almost like bribery. It's important as an organization to think through some guidelines about when hospitality can be given, and received. In general, as long as you declare what you are doing, this should be acceptable.

Hospitality is not about receiving back-handers. It is actually about getting your customers away from a normal situation, either their relationship with you or their work situation, so they can be more relaxed and talk to you about what they are actually looking for. There are a whole range of different hospitality options you can offer.

The following are just a couple of examples.

Christies, the international auction house, offers pre-auction dinners for major clients. This is a way of making the client feel special, and showing that you actually care about them. It can also be a really good way of getting to know customers better, and making a statement about them.

Rover Cars held a dinner party and champagne breakfast for 10,000 of its most valued customers to launch the new Range Rover at the Paris Motor Show. This wasn't about hard sell but was in fact making a comment about how Rover viewed its customers.

The company showed a three minute documentary commercial – again not hard sell – just showing pictures of the new Range Rover. There were people on hand to answer questions. They could alter the commercial according to the audience and had a number of different people who had driven Range Rovers talking about their experiences. The people featured on the video included Lord Lindsay, Richard Branson in the Cotswolds, and Robin Knox Johnson in Patagonia.

Over the following years many of these 10,000 customers either bought Range Rovers or recommended them to their friends. They became a kind of core customer club for Range Rover, and one they could go back to time and time again. The hospitality may have been expensive, but it has paid for itself time and time again, and made a clear comment about the way the company value its customers.

Of course there are many ways of organizing hospitality. Many companies now give days out for their top customers at many social calendar events, like Ascot and Wimbledon. Sporting events indeed have become a focus for corporate hospitality.

Hospitality is sometimes seen as a rather passive event. In other words, you simply take someone to an event that is taking place elsewhere.

What the Range Rover example shows is that sometimes putting on an event can be a powerful way of affirming your belief in your customers.

However, you don't need to concentrate on a large event like the Range Rover one. Small events can be equally persuasive and effective. For instance why not take a buyer out to dinner to celebrate 20 years of business together. You could also send congratulatory telegrams.

It's important to realize that the memory of such a surprise as this can actually last for a very long time. Often it's the unexpected invite or act of kindness to mark your respect for customers that can add real sparkle to a commercial and personal relationship.

Think International Rescue

Friendships are often tested when something goes wrong, or when someone is in trouble. In personal friendships people often look to their friends for a shoulder to cry on or indeed to help them out of a mess they have got themselves into. You may well be able to do similar things for your customers.

Customers can sometimes get themselves into a mess. They can sometimes run into trouble with a project or things can look like falling apart. Often these problems are nothing to do with you, and certainly nothing you have caused. However, if you can step in and help – even if you may not be able to charge for this service – you show a real commitment to them.

The following is a true story.

'I worked for a design company. One particular day they had a big pitch to present for a very important piece of work for the company. I received a phone call midway through the afternoon. It was hot, and I was settled into a piece of work at home that I needed to do. However, it was the director of the company who informed me that they had problems, they needed to get something out quickly, and they needed to get the proposal by the end of the day. He wondered was there anything I could do, or anyone I could suggest who could help?

I immediately put down my work and said I would be there in 45 minutes. I drove to their business, sat down, took out a pen, and wrote the proposal. In passing, one of the directors said how pleased they were, and it felt like International Rescue had actually stepped in to help. It was an act like this that frankly did disrupt my day, but which actually made a cast iron comment that I cared about the future of the business I was working with, and I cared about them as people.'

All too often people have a rather anodyne approach to business. But business is about relationships, and because it is about relationships, it's about emotions, about feelings, and about commitment to other people.

This means that if your customers get into trouble, and if you can be there to help them, then you will be remembered as the person who got them out of a hole. The one thing not to do is to help a customer out like this, and then send in a bill for a couple of hours work later on. It will absolutely destroy the relationship.

'THANKS FOR THE LIFT, LESTER'

There is a memorable story told about racing jockey Lester Piggott. In this story it is alleged that Lester Piggott was one day riding at a particular meeting, and he came across one of the commentators, who told him that his car had broken down, and he had to get on to the next race meeting where Piggott was also riding. Lester Piggott said it was fine, and that this particular commentator could come along with him in his helicopter. This was a delightful moment, and the commentator warmed towards him. He got the lift, and of course managed to fulfil his obligations.

About two weeks later a letter arrived at the commentator's house and in it was a bill for the helicopter flight. This may well not be true, but it's a good example of how not to dig someone out of a hole, and then dig yourself straight into one.

The training angle

We have looked throughout this book at the significance of staff in delivering that all-important special relationship with customers. You may well find that your staff are naturally able to build up a relationship approach with customers.

However, many staff have either had this ability:

- knocked out of them – they have been told they have to be 'professional' or 'aloof'
- worn down by overwork
- corrupted by their fellow employees.

In these kind of instances you need to put in place a training scheme that will help your staff become the customer's friend. This kind of training scheme is relatively common in sales-oriented organizations, but less common in other kinds of organization. The cornerstones of any such training scheme are:

1. Looking at the hearts and minds issues. Some organizations are deliberately bringing in customers to talk to staff about what it feels like to be a customer. They may well ask the staff to act out role play so they play the part of customers, to get a chance to walk about in customer shoes.
2. Concrete skills. In order to play a full part in getting to know customers better, there are a number of concrete skills you may need to learn. For instance assertiveness, telephone skills, etc.
3. Know your product. You need to know about your product. It's very difficult to strike up a relationship with customers if you don't know your product in detail. The more you know about the product, the more you can offer, and you can then play a more equal part in the relationship. We have all come across examples when we have been in a restaurant or the like and have asked about what wine goes well with a particular meal, only to find the waiter or waitress having to scurry off to find someone else.

   Empowered organizations empower their staff with knowledge, and it is knowledge about the service and about the product you are offering that allows staff to play a fuller role with customers.

Magazines

Magazines are tried and tested, and can be extremely effective in terms of building relationships. We have looked at the way Heinz have used their magazine to break away from traditional advertising routes. Many companies are now sending out magazines. It's for this reason that to really make a magazine work you need to be different. One of the most effective ways of making magazines count is to make customers feel that by reading the magazine they are joining a kind of interest group or club. Many companies have developed these.

Pedigree Chum now offer magazines for dog owners explaining tips and tricks for looking after different breeds of dog and the particular kinds of food these dogs prefer. However, it isn't just big companies. The following example shows how one small company developed an amazing magazine that helped lock in customers to its way of thinking.

Case study

COSMETICS TO GO

Cosmetics To Go were a small cosmetics mail order company based in Poole in Dorset. They sold a range of rather weird and wonderful products with extraordinary names. Their products were all environmentally friendly, and generally quirky. The company reflected this with a magazine sent out to all its mail order customers.

The magazine included photos of various employees and customers, and also included poems from customers about different products, cartoons, and some genuinely entertaining stories. At the end of every couple of pages there would be a coupon or an order form, to order the products.

Customers used to really look forward to receiving the magazine for a read. It wasn't just put straight in the bin. In fact it became something that people would read and then leave around, and maybe chuckle at, and certainly at the end of the day make an order from. Above all the magazine worked because it absolutely reflected the company values and gave an entertaining diversion for customers. Customers are generally not stupid and are not very interested about reading about internal issues about a company.

This Cosmetics To Go magazine managed to be of the same kind of quality as the interest magazines you would buy in a newsagent.

So, only provide a magazine if it can be different and if it can interest customers. Otherwise it's likely to be a waste of trees.

Offering something unique to customers

Clubs

Many organizations are now running clubs. Clubs can be a very effective way of building customer loyalty and making customers feel part of the company. They are also a good way of identifying people you can keep in touch with, and building up that all-important relationship over time.

In the introduction to this book we looked at the Pepsi Max Club offer to youngsters. It isn't just youngsters however who are being offered clubs. For instance, an example of a club is Air Miles. Air Miles offer additional incentives such as a dining club where you can cash in your Air Miles at various restaurants. The best customers may even be invited to dinner with British Airways executives, for instance.

THE CASA BUITONI CLUB

Nestle the Swiss food giant has signed up around 80,000 customers to the Casa Buitoni Club quarterly special interest magazine and activities for consumers who want to 'share a love of Italian cooking'(people who have 5 times above the national average pasta consumption). There are recipes, articles, special offers, competitions (eg win cooking holiday in beautiful Tuscan villa). Members have increased purchases by 15 per cent since the launch of the club in 1993 although the brand total sales have fallen due to the impact of own label products. However, Nestle believe the club will pay for itself in the long term.

These are just a couple of examples of clubs but the most important thing is to think about the club mentality.

People enjoy being members of clubs and it's much easier to get to know people over time if they are members of your club. What many organizations and departments are now doing is thinking of ways of making people feel a part of what they are doing. And clubs are one of the ways of allowing people to see you are offering a prestige product and that they can belong. In other words they can get a slice of the action.

Gifts

American Express cardholders who frequently dine in a particular restaurant (and pay with their card) may get a free bottle of wine courtesy of AMEX. The gift is appropriate and matches the means and interests of the customer.

This can be taken one step further with closed loop marketing. AMEX brings other hotels, shops and restaurants into the relationship by providing them with information about customers who have shopped with them using AMEX. This allows them to make their own special offers to AMEX users direct.

Mark Stevens Loyalty Manager of AMEX explains that

> *'if I get value from you I am prepared to give back value to you. As long as it's net-net that's fine'.*

Gifts and incentives need to be handled with care. Give only what is appropriate. Perhaps one of the most famous disasters was the Hoover flights promotion. Hoover offered free flights to a destination of your choice for every £100 spent on Hoover products. Customers were ecstatic. They rushed out to buy vacuum cleaners and washing machines they didn't even need, because it was cheaper than buying the flights. Ultimately Hoover could not fulfil their promise and tried to persuade customers they had misread the small print. The customers took Hoover to court.

This inappropriate incentive cost Hoover millions. Loyal customers left them for life.

Are your gifts appropriate? Try the following test.

The Wow! test

How will your customer react when they receive a gift or invitation to reward their long standing custom? Choose the answer which you think applies best and read on.

That's nice. They're happy, but have you made an impression? Think again about what you gave? Are they really interested? Is it too tacky ...?

That's great. A happy customer. The gift has struck the right note, made them feel happy, but hasn't taken their breathe away.

Wow! Have you done too much? Sending a jewel encrusted token to a household customer who has loyally bought your cornflakes for 20 years is going too far.

Loyalty cards

A quarter of American consumers are now linked into some form of frequent shopper programme. Customers' spending patterns now indicate that free gifts are less of an incentive than value for money. Good value keeps the customer coming back for more.

Petrol stations such as Mobil have run such schemes for years. Glove boxes all over the land are exploding with tumblers! Now other retail outlets are setting up similar schemes.

Tesco's were the first major UK supermarket chain to launch a loyalty card. The scheme was in part a response to customer comments about the inconvenience of money off coupons. Customers receive points for every £10 spent which are logged on a purpose-made credit card. After a set period of time points can be redeemed against future bills. Spend more, pay less in the end.

Sainsburys, despite initial doubts voiced by Chairman David Sainsbury, have followed suit, extending the scheme after a successful test period in their main branches.

That extra little something

Often it doesn't take much to make a customer feel special – a simple thank you or passing note helps. This is what some companies do :

- three figure donors to major land purchase funds for the RSPB receive certificates, signed by the chairman or personality fronting the campaign, acknowledging their contribution. A nice but simple momento for the wall
- Sheba (Pedigree Pet Foods) send birthday cards to cats who eat their pet food ... via their owners, just in case moggy can't tear the envelope open!
- many companies choose Christmas to say that extra little thank you. Calendars and desk diaries proliferate but it pays to be original.

Sponsorship and charity links

■ ■ ■

Most successful charities will agree that supporting charity makes sound business sense. Jeremy White, the Chief Executive of the Prince's Youth Business Trust, believes that companies should invest money wisely in our communities to benefit us all.

Lodwrick Cook, chairman of ARCO (one of the US's leading companies, and a great corporate philanthropist), gives the following explanation of why it makes sense :

> *'First consumers like it: a company that cares for the community in which customers work and live improves its reputation and strengthens brand loyalty. Second, employees like it : a company's most able staff are also the most mobile. People want to be associated with an employer that has a caring reputation and community commitment strengthens employee loyalty. Third, participating positively in society improves the welfare of everyone.'*

Companies generally chose to support charities which are relevant to their customers and the customers' interests.

- Cadbury's run the annual Cadbury's Buttons Strollerthon. All the family (including toddlers in pushchairs) are encouraged to join this sponsored walk along the Thames to raise funds for the NSPCC

- Hamleys linked up with the National Deaf Children's Association running a series of activities and promotions through Christmas including a signing Santa in their Regent Street store
- Barclays Bank have for several years supported New Stages, a festival which brings fringe theatre productions by exciting new companies to the provinces ie the regions where Barclays have customers.

Charity begins at home

Support for local issues is particularly relevant when it comes to stakeholders. Companies can develop a closer relationship with local customers by getting involved in community events or helping with important local issues.

Support for local charities can help to counteract bad impressions created by noise or pollution from a factory. Simply being a large local employer or service industry, can mean that the community expects the company's support for local hospices or environmental campaigns. These issues are more relevant to a company's stakeholders than, for example, funding a major opera production.

FORD

The Ford Motor Company took this approach in Essex. Fundraising activities organized by the staff are encouraged – it's a great team builder. The company also regularly support a local hospice, St Luke's, with gifts in kind. The hospice get their pick of secondhand furniture from office moves or staff relocation.

A few years ago the Dagenham Ford car plant hit the headlines with an innovative environmental project. The factory was surrounded by unsightly derelict land. Staff decided it was a good idea to encourage wildlife to use the land. They linked up with local environmental groups to transform it. The project involved local schools and social groups as well as Ford staff, and attracted a great deal of local media interest. The project took a great deal of hard work, and financial support from the Head Office, but the end result was a stunning wildlife reserve which could be enjoyed by staff and locals, most of whom were also customers. The project won an innovation award from the environmental group the Groundwork Trust.

Some companies like their managers to take on this responsibility in a more personal way. McDonald's encourages their managers to get involved in the community by becoming school governors. The rationale is that managers then play an active part in the community where they work and will be seen as responsible and caring members of that community. So McDonald's itself becomes a company at the heart of the community. Think about it – where would you rather take your children for a Saturday afternoon treat? The local burger bar? Or the McDonald's run by Tom, that nice chap who is always so helpful at the school PTA meetings.

Managers at Allied Brewers are encouraged to join in local charity events or get involved in neighbourhood watch schemes. The principle is the same. The managers get known as active community members first of all, and the reputation rubs off on the company for which they work. He's a good chap – it must be a nice company.

A health warning

Charity can, however, go too far. Customers will not appreciate unbecoming links – it may even put them off you for life.

British Sugar decided to sponsor a series of books in schools. A laudable idea, but the text encouraged children to add sugar to drinks to give them extra energy. Apart from infuriating the British Dental Association, the suggestion came to the attention of the press and caused public outrage.

Some companies are accused of paying blood money to charities to salve their consciences. Support which helps rectify the problems a company may have caused is again laudable, but needs to be carefully pitched.

Shell UK have for many years supported a number of environmental projects. Special promotions have met with the approval of the consumer. Plans to scrap the Brent Spar oil rig, however, changed the consumer's mind. Customers boycotted Shell petrol stations across Europe – with particular fervour in Holland and Germany, where more than 2000 protest letters and phone calls were received in one day alone. A Dutch company, Shell felt unable to totally ignore the views of its customers and were forced to reverse their decision to scrap the rig at sea.

The round up

Well, you've seen a whole range of ideas and tips in this section for developing a broad relationship with customers.

Some of these have been simple, others more long term and complicated. They all have in common the need to stay in touch and develop bonds with customers that last.

So ... what next?

Now it's just a question of doing something about it. And that needs careful planning and thought.

The trouble with the subject of a book like this one is that it can strike a real chord and get everyone very excited. But, slow down. It's very likely that the amount you can do personally, without getting clearance from someone else, or without taking resources from other core business activities, is limited. It's also inevitable that the areas you may want to tackle involve other people, their attitudes, beliefs and approach.

Also, there's a simple truth that says, success breeds success. Too many people set themselves sky-high targets and then fail to reach them. Disappointment sets in and any progress that could have been made is lost.

So, our advice is to draw up an action plan, taking account of the following questions before you start:

- what are the 20 per cent of things I could tackle that might affect 80 per cent of my customers?
- which things can I start without having to get approval from someone else, or go through a very long-winded process of writing reports and making proposals?
- which activities will cost me least and achieve the best returns?
- which ones are practical, achievable and realistic?
- what could I achieve in a reasonable time scale, so we can see real progress being made?
- what have I felt, as I read the book, were the most appropriate things for me to try?

Once you've asked and answered these – and any other relevant questions that occur to you – pick something to tackle, something you really believe in.

Then set yourself some objectives. Decide how the situation will look when you've achieved what you want to do, and quantify it so you have clear targets and some way of measuring progress.

The chances are that this will mean getting other people involved as well. There's very little in this book that you can do alone, unless you count activities like getting other people excited, committed and trained.

And now comes the hardest step of all to take, wherein lies the heart of learning to love your customers. It is ... take no action; stop, think; reflect.

Developing a customer relationship isn't a series of quick fixes, posters and slogans that you can slap on a wall to say how wonderful customers are and how much you love them. You know this, for yourself. It's bigger, deeper and more important than that. It's about a fundamental belief in the importance of people to your organization, both the ones who work in it and the ones who are served by it.

So the first step to take is to spend a fair amount of time mulling over what you have either discovered or confirmed about customers and how your organization does and should treat them.

Then go out and play your part in the customer revolution.

Index